LET'S HAVE A PARTY

By

MILDRED DOOLEY CATHCART

MOODY PRESS
CHICAGO

Printed in the United States of America

CONTENTS

3

LET'S HAVE A PARTY

IN THE BOOK OF PROVERBS we read: "A merry heart maketh a cheerful countenance. . . . A merry heart doeth good like a medicine." It is a good thing to be happy in the Lord, to come together and rejoice so long as we do those things which are well-pleasing unto Him.

It is with this thought in mind that I have prepared the party suggestions in this book.

I believe that we should work and pray together as a family. I think too we should play together as a family. So I have prepared games which are suitable and adaptable to various age groups. Many of the preparations are simple enough so that the smaller children can actually have a hand in the festivities.

God has promised that where two or three are gathered together in His name, He is there. I have planned the type of entertainment which will honor Him. When you write your invitations you might suggest that your guests bring along their Bibles as they will need them for some of the games. It is also well to close your parties with a hymn and benediction.

Poetically we have planned:

> Games for thought
> Games for fun,
> Games to suit
> Just everyone!

I am indebted to our two daughters, Kerry Lee and Jean Marie, who helped me prepare many of the games and who so willingly "tested" them for me. We have had fun!

We hope that you will have fun too as you plan your party.

—MILDRED DOOLEY CATHCART

A NEW YEAR'S PARTY—"RING IN THE NEW"

They sang as it were a new song!

GETTING FRIENDS TOGETHER to welcome the New Year is one of the jolliest and easiest ways to entertain.

Since you are "ringing in" the New Year, use the bell theme for this party.

INVITATIONS

Fold dark construction paper in half, cut out a bell, and sprinkle the outside bell with gilt. Blow a bit of artificial snow on it to add sparkle. Open the bell and write your invitation on the inside. As a suggestion, you might write:

> We'll ring out the Old Year,
> We'll ring in the New;
> We have a wee bell
> Just waiting for you.

Then include the place, time, and date of your party.

DECORATIONS

Little decorating is necessary for a New Year's party since the Christmas decorations are still in use. However, have your door decorated with a chain of bells and have bells displayed prominently throughout the house.

Use a little hand bell to ring when you wish to gain the attention of your guests.

Just before the bells ring out the Old Year, give each guest a paper bag containing such items as confetti, noisemakers, paper hats, and balloons. Be sure to include a small bell so each person may help to "Ring out the old—ring in the new."

6

Your refreshments can bear out the "ring in" theme too. Cut sandwiches with a bell-shaped cooky cutter and decorate to resemble bells. Cookies may be bells decorated with various colored icings. If you have bell-shaped pans, use them for baking cakes or molding salads. Decorate cupcakes with white icing and outline bells in red or green. If you serve ice cream, order it with a bell frozen through the center.

New Year's tradition demands the Wassail or punch bowl. Surround this bowl with sprigs of holly or evergreen. Add a gay red ribbon to which attach several small bells.

If you have nut cups, tie a tiny bell to each. Place cards may have tiny gold bells attached to one corner with red or green ribbon.

GAMES

Ring the Bell

Cut from construction paper 20 white bells, 15 green, 10 blue, 5 gold. (Increase the number of bells for a large group.) Before your guests arrive, hide these bells about the room. At a given signal, the players are to hunt the bells. Allow various points for the different colors: a white bell counts one point; a green, two points; a blue one, three points; but each golden bell adds ten points. The person having the most points is winner.

What Time Is It?

Place a clock before all the guests and tell them they must be able to identify the parts of a clock correctly. These Bible references will help them name the various parts of the clock. (Perhaps you should mention on the invitations that each guest is to bring his Bible.)

1. Proverbs 10:13 _____   (Back)
2. Ecclesiastes 12:6 _____   (Wheel)
3. Fourth book of the Bible _____ (Numbers)
4. Job 5:6 _____   (Spring)

7

5. Exodus 5:19 _____ (Case)
6. Ezra 7:9 _____ (Hand)
7. Revelation 4:6 _____ (Crystal)
8. Malachi 3:17 _____ (Jewels)
9. Psalm 27:9 _____ (Face)
10. Romans 13:11 _____ (Time)

At What Time?

Each of the following questions may be answered with a time of day.

1. At what time did Adam and Eve hear the voice of the Lord in the garden? _____ (In the cool of the day)
2. At what time did Isaac go into the field to meditate? _____ (At eventide)
3. At what time did the ten virgins hear the cry of the bridegroom? _____ (At midnight)
4. At what time did the women come to the sepulcher of Jesus? _____ (Very early in the morning)
5. At what time did Nicodemus come to Jesus? _____ (At night)
6. At what time did Judas depart after Jesus had told of His betrayal? _____ (It was night)
7. At what time did Jesus feed the multitude? _____ (It was evening)
8. At what time is it said, "It will be foul weather today: for the sky is red and lowering"? _____ (In the morning)
9. At what time did Jesus cry: "My God, my God, why hast thou forsaken me?" _____ (About the ninth hour)
10. At what time were shepherds keeping watch over their flock? _____ (At night)
11. At what time did He come to the temple to teach? _____ (Early in the morning)
12. At what time did Paul come to Damascus? _____ (At noon)

Time Marches On

All players are seated in a circle and each one is given a certain time—such as one o'clock or one-thirty. The leader walks around the circle calling out various times. As each person's time is called, he must follow the leader. When the leader finally says, "Time marches on," all try to be seated. The one left standing becomes It.

Stop the Clock

This is a stunt strictly for fun and not to be tolerated if your guests are dignified. Notify your guests that during the evening at various intervals the alarm will ring. Each person is to stop immediately and hold the position he happens to be in until the alarm quits ringing. You will find most hilarious and unusual predicaments.

Keeping Up with the Times

Before your party, search through old newspapers and magazines for pictures of people who have been prominent through the year. Cut the heads and paste them on different bodies. By exchanging the faces, you will be surprised how difficult it is to identify the persons correctly.

The Clock Strikes Midnight

Make a large clock face on heavy cardboard and print the hours with black crayola. Choose sides and give each team a penny or small object to toss at the clock. Each player may have a certain number of turns and his score will be the hour he strikes. If the tossed object does not fall upon the clock there is no score. If the penny strikes "midnight" add 20 to the score.

After the guests have "rung in" the New Year, have them gather around the piano and sing some favorite hymns; and before they depart, all may repeat the benediction from Numbers 6:24-27:

9

The Lord bless thee and keep thee;
The Lord make his face shine upon thee, and be gracious
unto thee;
The Lord lift up his countenance upon thee, and give
thee peace.

Amen.

A Good Resolution

It would be a fine thing to make a resolution to read daily
God's Word. There are many things God tells us about His
Word. See who can find them first.

1. _____ of the Word—James 1:23
2. _____ of the Word—James 1:22
3. _____ the Word—II Timothy 4:2
4. _____ the words—Acts 20:35
5. _____ the Word—Mark 4:14
6. _____ in the Word—Galatians 6:6
7. _____ _____ the Word—Philippians 2:16
8. _____ up in the words—I Timothy 4:6
9. _____ His Word—Titus 1:3
10. _____ in the Word—I Timothy 5:17
11. _____ the good Word—Hebrews 6:5
12. _____ My Word—Revelation 3:8
13. _____ for the Word—Revelation 6:9
14. _____ the Word—Matthew 8:8
15. _____ My Word—John 5:24

ANSWERS

1. Hearer	6. Taught	11. Tasted
2. Doers	7. Holding forth	12. Kept
3. Preach	8. Nourished	13. Slain
4. Remember	9. Manifested	14. Speak
5. Soweth	10. Labor	15. Heareth

A NEW YEAR'S PARTY—WATCH
THE CLOCK

Invitations

SINCE TIME is the theme of a watch party, we shall make these invitations in the form of an hourglass. Cut two hourglasses from a flat sheet of plastic and seal them together with a hot knife, leaving a small opening at the top for a few grains of fine sand. (Corn meal will do if no sand is available.) Now seal top end firmly. Paste the hourglass inside a folded sheet of heavy paper and cut out a portion of the front cover so that the hourglass shows. Write your invitation inside the booklet. Your verse may be similar to this:

> The sands of time are slipping fast,
> The Old Year's nearly gone;
> But let us get together, and
> We'll greet the New Year with a song.

Decorations

Your Christmas decorations will suffice for this party too, but have a few clocks in conspicuous places. Set the alarms for different times so they will ring throughout the evening.

Make a large hourglass similar to the ones in your invitations and place it on the front door to greet your guests.

When you are timing your players for certain games an inexpensive hourglass "egg timer" would be fun to use. These might be used for prizes, too.

Refreshments

Remember the *time* theme in preparing your refreshments. If you have sandwiches, prepare a few round openfaced ones to resemble clocks. Spread the sandwich with cream cheese and form numerals of bits of olives, pickles, or pimento. Cookies may be decorated to resemble clocks also.

A large "clock cake" makes a most attractive centerpiece for the table. Place it on a footed cake plate. Run tiny narrow ribbon streamers from the twelve numerals. In a circle around the cake arrange twelve little figurines to represent each month of the year. One streamer will lead to a snowman for January; another to a heart for February; to a shamrock for March; to a bunny for April; to a basket for May; to a bride for June; to a flag for July; to a tiny picnic basket for August; to a book for September; to a pumpkin for October; to a turkey for November; to a Christmas tree for December.

Place cards may have hourglasses or clocks drawn on them. Place nut cups on a larger circle with clock numerals around the edge.

If you want a more artistic centerpiece, fashion a clock out of real or artificial flowers. Draw a heavy circle on the table, cover with white flowers, then use colored flowers to form numerals and hands. Real flowers might be similarly arranged in a low round dish.

GAMES

What Time Is It?

Before the guests arrive hide a number of heavy cardboard clocks about the room, each bearing different hours. At a given signal the players begin searching for the clocks. When time is called, each player turns in his clocks. The one who comes closest to having all the hours from one to twelve is winner.

The game may be varied by having each player add up his hours, a prize to be given to the one with the highest total of hours.

Turning Back the Hands of Time

Instruct each person to bring along a baby picture of himself. Arrange them on a table, number each, and see who can identify the largest number correctly.

Time Bomb

Put a prize in a box and wrap it securely. Then print a note giving instructions to do some stunt. Wrap another layer of paper around this and place note on top for another stunt. Keep adding enough notes so each guest will unwrap a stunt. Draw a clock on the package, informing the players that this is a time bomb and they must get rid of it as soon as possible. Players hand the package from one to another. You set an alarm to ring every few seconds. The person holding the package when the alarm sounds, unwraps the first layer of paper and does his stunt. This goes on until each has his turn at unwrapping. The last person "gets the bomb." He is fooled to find a really useful prize!

A New Time

The Bible tells us that there are many *new* things for God's people. Use your Bible to find what they are.

1. When we are in Christ we are a *new* _____
   II Corinthians 5:17
2. He has given us a *new* _____ John 13:34
3. We can sing unto Him a *new* _____ Psalm 33:3
4. When we are baptized, we should walk in a *new* _____ _____ Romans 6:4
5. We read of a *new* and _____ Hebrews 10:20
6. We are promised a *new* _____ and a *new* _____ Ezekiel 36:26
7. There will be a *new* _____ and a *new* _____ Revelation 21:1

ANSWERS

1. Creature
2. Commandment
3. Song
4. Life

5. Living way
6. Heart and spirit
7. Heaven and earth

13

New Year's Resolutions

This is the time to begin our new resolutions. Ask each player to write the letters of his first and last names on different lines of the sheet. Then have them write what happened when they tried to *keep* their resolutions. Only each word must begin with the letters of his name. Mine might read like this:

Mine Is Less Difficult Remembering Each Day.
Can't Always Tell Him "Come" at Right Time.

Of course, the answers will be silly! That is the object of the game.

Who Made This Resolution?

Have each person write his New Year's resolution on a slip of paper. Collect the papers, read the resolutions, and see if the listeners can identify the writers.

A SNOW MAN PARTY

WHEN A LOVELY SNOW covers the ground it is time to go "Dashing through the snow in a one-horse open sleigh." What could be more fun than a sleigh ride, a skating party, or a coasting party? You might like to bring the gang in for a chili supper afterward. Or follow your outdoor activities with a party at your home. What then could be more appropriate than a jolly Snow Man party?

INVITATIONS

For a Snow Man party, a jolly snow man is a *must* for your invitations. Use white construction paper and cut out snow men. Black crayon may outline the features. Tiny sequins or buttons may be glued on for coat buttons. Tie a tiny ribbon scarf about his neck. Cut a construction paper broom and tuck under his arm. The broom will carry the invitation. If you wish to be more realistic, cover the snow man with cotton. A rhyming invitation might say:

> This jolly little Snow man,
>   Has come with word so gay:
> "Come and have some fun with me
>   Before I melt away."

DECORATIONS

Wouldn't it be ideal to greet your guests with a jolly snow man standing near the door? Build a large snow man and place across him a banner saying "Welcome."

If the weather permits, and you are entertaining children, you might let each build a small snow man before he comes indoors. A small prize could be given for the best snow man.

Use green and white streamers with silver icicles hanging from them. Jolly little snow men should hang in the doorways.

For your table, a green cloth with tiny white paper snow-flakes cut from lace paper doilies will look attractive. If you wish, use a white cloth and scatter tiny sprigs of evergreen about. Make the greenery sparkle by spraying it with artificial snow.

A Snow Man centerpiece is certainly a necessity for this party. An oatmeal carton may form the body. Cover the box with white crepe paper but first pad the carton with soft cloth or cotton for extra plumpness. Stuff a ball-shaped piece of paper for the head. Paste cotton over the entire snow man and sprinkle with artificial snow to give a more realistic appearance. Make a tall black hat from construction paper and add a gay scarf. Use shiny bits of coal for the eyes and mouth and roll up a piece of orange paper (carrot shaped) for the nose. Tie broomstraws to a small stick to make him a broom.

Place the snow man on a "mirror" lake. You can make trees by painting spools green and sticking sprigs of evergreen in them. Place these around the snow man and add a few reindeer or other tiny animals in your "forest."

Place a circle of snow men candles around the larger snow man. If this is a party honoring someone's birthday, light the candles and sing "Happy Birthday." You will find these lighted candles add a fairy-like touch to the snow scene if you light the candles and turn out the other lights when the guests come into the dining room.

Individual snow men may be made by using two marsh-mallows for the body and a gumdrop for the head. A tooth-pick will hold them together. Cloves make the features. Add paper hats and bright red ribbon scarfs. You can also make snow men of popcorn using larger balls for the body and a smaller one for the head. Use pieces of black and red gum-drops for the features.

REFRESHMENTS

If you and your friends have spent the evening out in the cold, you will enjoy chili soup, hot chocolate, or hot dogs.

Take your guests into the kitchen and let them help "serve" themselves.

If you plan another type of refreshment, you will find various ways to carry out your color scheme. Cheese spreads may be tinted pale green. Use bits of olive or pimento in chicken salad for color. Salads and desserts may be made with lime gelatin base. Frost cupcakes with green and white icing and decorate. Cut cookies in the shape of snow men. Ice cream may be obtained green and white. Tint coconut pale green to use for toppings and frostings.

GAMES

Throwing Snowballs

Stuff a small white sack to represent a snowball. Stand up a snow man made of heavy cardboard and see who can knock him down with a snowball. Each person or team has a certain number of throws.

White as a Snow Man

A snow man is very white but the Bible tells of other things that are white. How many of these do you know?

1. "The house of Israel called the name thereof _____; and it was like coriander seed, white." (Manna)
2. "And the cloud departed from off the tabernacle and, behold, _____ became leprous, white as snow." (Miriam)
3. "Let thy _____ be always white." (Garments)
4. "Thou canst not make one _____ white or black." (Hair)
5. "His face did shine as the sun, and his _____ was white as the light." (Raiment)
6. "Lift up your eyes, and look on the _____; for they are white already to harvest." (Fields)
7. "While they looked steadfastly toward heaven two men stood by them in white _____." (Apparel)

17

8. "To him that overcometh will I give to eat of the hidden manna, and will give him a white _____." (Stone)

9. "And I saw a great white _____ and him that sat on it." (Throne)

10. "Woe unto you, scribes and Pharisees, hypocrites! for ye are like unto whited _____." (Sepulchers)

Making a Snow Man

Give each player paper and pencil and then blindfold each one. See who can draw the best snow man. For older groups provide a fruit jar for the body, cotton, crepe paper, buttons, paper, scissors, and paste, and see who can make the most realistic snow man.

Shoveling Snow

Snowflakes (paper cut fine) are placed in piles about the room. Each player is equipped with a teaspoon and a container. He is to shovel up his pile of snow *but* he can use only one hand. If youngsters are playing, provide each with a tiny sandpile shovel and pail. These will make useful "take home" gifts.

The Snow Man Runs Away

Frosty, the snow man ran away. Some people in Bible stories have run away too. Can you match these correctly?

1. He fled from his father-in-law.	a. Judas
2. He fled in a ship.	b. Ruth
3. She fled with her son.	c. Jacob
4. He ran from Potiphar's wife	d. Elijah
5. She left her land to become a bride.	e. Joseph
6. He left his sheep to fight a giant.	f. David
7. He left a king's palace to join his people.	g. Rebekah
8. She left her country with her mother-in-law.	h. Jonah
9. He left by a chariot of fire.	i. Moses
10. He departed and hanged himself.	j. Hagar

18

ANSWERS

1—c	3—j	5—g	7—i	9—d
2—h	4—e	6—f	8—b	10—a

Melting the Snow Man

Give each player paper and pencil and see who can make the most words from the phrase *"Snow man melts."*

A Bible Snow Quiz

Snow is mentioned many times in the Bible. How many of these questions can you answer?

1. What did Benaiah slay in the time of snow? II Samuel 23:20 _____
2. What was snow covered? Jeremiah 18:14 _____
3. He giveth snow like what? Psalm 147:16 _____
4. For what is she not afraid of snow? Proverbs 31:21 _____
5. What did the Ancient of days have that was white as snow? Daniel 7:9 _____
6. Who is said to be like the cold of snow in the time of harvest? Proverbs 25:13 _____
7. Snow comes in what season in this verse? Proverbs 26:1 _____
8. What shall be as white as snow? Isaiah 1:18 _____
9. Whose raiment was white as snow? Matthew 28:2, 3 _____

ANSWERS

1. Lion
2. Lebanon
3. Wool
4. Household
5. Garment
6. A faithful messenger
7. Summer
8. Your sins
9. The angel of the Lord

White As Snow

Players form a circle. When It points at a player and counts five, the player must name a white object. If he fails, he becomes It.

A HEART PARTY

A merry heart maketh a cheerful countenance.

I T IS EASY ENOUGH to put your "heart" into this party, and
the more the merrier. A heart seems to be the accepted
symbol for Valentine's Day, and red or pink and white are
the accepted colors, so plan your party around these.

INVITATIONS

Your invitations will be heart-shaped, of course, and may
be white hearts with red ink or vice versa. For lacy effects,
use paper lace doilies and bright flowers for decorating or
add designs cut from magazines. You might begin your fun
with the invitation. Cut the heart into large jig-saw pieces
so the recipient will have to put it together to read your note.
For an invitation you might write:

> Here is my heart,
> Broken in two;
> Put it together
> For a message for you!

DECORATIONS AND REFRESHMENTS

Choose red and white or pink and white streamers from
which suspend frilly little hearts. Your doorways may have
streamers of tiny hearts hanging in them. If you have bright
red geraniums in bloom tie a red and white ribbon around
the flower pots and use these flowers in strategic spots. Decorate your windows or curtains with tiny gay hearts.

Your table will look attractive if you use a plain white
cover and then make large red hearts for place mats. Use
plain white dishes to show up plainly on the red hearts.

There are many attractive Valentine party centerpieces. Choose the one best suited to the age group you are entertaining. A bouquet of red and white flowers between red candles is effective. For children a plastic tree whose branches hold red and white gumdrops will look as good as they taste.

As people of all ages enjoy a valentine exchange, ask each guest to bring a valentine or provide a valentine favor for each. What could be more appropriate for a centerpiece than a lovely valentine box? Start with a plain box, add several rows of crepe paper ruffles, tiny hearts, and cupids; then attach one end of a gay white and red streamer to a valentine and the other to each plate so each may draw out a valentine. Make the box as elaborate as you wish but remember to have it low enough so the guests can see over it.

There seems to be no limit to things you can prepare for refreshments. Heart-shaped open-faced sandwiches, heart-shaped cookies, salads, or cakes made in heart-shaped molds, or ice cream with a red heart frozen through the center will look most "heart-y."

For an unusual valentine cake, bake your favorite three-layered white cake and put together with fluffy boiled frosting. On the top place a very firm gelatin red heart. (Use only 1¼ cups of water when setting gelatin). Cover the outside of the cake with frosting and add mounds of coconut.

Place cards and favors may be combined for this party. For the children, make a large paper heart, cut two slits through it, and insert a red sucker or stick candy. Teen-agers will prefer inexpensive pencils or other favors. The ladies will be pleased to find a corsage on their place card.

For prizes, select items that come in red or white, such as balloons, pencils, handkerchiefs, stationery, or other items wrapped in white paper and decorated with hearts.

GAMES
Your Heart Will Tell

Hide various colored hearts about the room. Most of them will be red. Each person is to find all the red ones he can and then find just *one* of any other color. A prize may be given to the one finding the most red hearts. Then seat the players and tell their fortunes with the colored hearts. Make up your own ideas, but to start you off, here are a few suggestions: a white heart indicates you will become a doctor (for adults you may say he will soon meet a doctor) ; a gold heart indicates money soon to come your way; a purple heart foretells an encounter with royalty; blue means you are soon to go on a trip via the airplane; green means you will live on a farm; pink means that very soon you will receive a gift.

Bottle up Your Heart

Each player has five small candy hearts which he tries to drop into a milk bottle or toss into a shallow pan. You may make this more difficult by blindfolding the player after giving him a good look at the bottle or pan.

Making a Broken Heart Well

Cut large red hearts into jig-saw puzzles. For youngsters these must be fairly simple. For adults you may make the puzzles more difficult and let the players work in teams, putting the hearts together.

I Lost My Heart

Players form a circle and the first begins by saying, "I lost my heart in—" and he names a city beginning with the letter *A*. The second repeats the phrase but names a city beginning with *B*. Each player who fails to name a place must drop out of the game.

How Many Hearts?

Hide a great many letters which are needed to spell out the word *heart*. Allow the players a given time to hunt for letters—no trading or giving away. When time is called ask them to be seated and see who can spell the word *heart* the largest number of times with the letters he has found.

A Bible Quiz

1. "Making _____ in your heart to the Lord." (Melody)
2. "The heart is _____ above all things." (Deceitful)
3. "Blessed are the _____ in heart for they shall see God." (Pure)
4. "The Lord is nigh unto them that are of a _____ heart." (Broken)
5. "Keep thy heart with all _____." (Diligence)
6. "Create in me a _____ heart, O God." (Clean)
7. "_____ which strengtheneth man's heart." (Bread)
8. "Search me, O God, and _____ my heart." (Know)
9. "They have more than heart could _____." (Wish)
10. "A _____ heart is sin." (Proud)
11. "O fools, and _____ of heart to believe." (Slow)
12. "But _____ kept all these things and pondered them in her heart." (Mary)

Drawing with All Your Heart

Give each player a sheet of paper on which you have drawn a fairly large-sized heart. Using this as a basis, tell each one to see who can draw the best picture in just five minutes.

A Puzzle

The first of letters in each name,
(Just toss the others away)
Will give you all the needed signs
Of Valentine's Day.

He'd kill the Child of God's delight. _____ (Herod)
He left in chariot so bright. _____ (Elijah)
He lived in a garden so wondrously fine. _____ (Adam)
Jacob worked; then said, "She's mine." _____ (Rachel)
When only a child, the Scriptures he knew. _____ (Timothy)
He saw a light; heard God's voice too. _____ (Saul)

Hunt a Heart

Children "of all ages" enjoy a heart hunt. Hide small paper hearts, and score so many points for various colored ones. Candy hearts may be hidden, and the highest score goes to the one having largest number with certain quotations.

Name a Pair

Give the first word of a famous pair of articles and have the person add the second word. Among famous pairs you might include:

1. Pen_____ (Ink)
2. Paper_____ (Pencil)
3. Bacon_____ (Eggs)
4. Salt_____ (Pepper)
5. Night_____ (Day)
6. Black_____ (White)
7. Adam_____ (Eve)
8. Thunder_____ (Lightning)
9. Bread_____ (Butter)
10. Boots_____ (Saddle)
11. P's_____ (Q's)
12. Cup_____ (Saucer)
13. Ice cream_____ (Cake)
14. Horse_____ (Buggy)
15. Stop_____ (Go)
16. Needle_____ (Thread)

Famous Pairs

Match the husbands and wives.

			Answers:
1. Adam	a. Ruth	_____	(1—d)
2. Abraham	b. Jochebed	_____	(2—h)
3. Isaac	c. Zipporah	_____	(3—j)
4. Boaz	d. Eve	_____	(4—a)
5. Elkanah	e. Asenath	_____	(5—g)
6. Moses	f. Esther	_____	(6—c)
7. Joseph	g. Hannah	_____	(7—e)
8. Amram	h. Sarah	_____	(8—b)
9. Ahasuerus	i. Mary	_____	(9—f)
10. Joseph	j. Rebekah	_____	(10—i)

Make a Valentine

Provide guests with construction paper, lace, scissors, lace doilies, paste, scraps of ribbon, and see who can make the prettiest valentine. The children might like to take their valentines home to Mother. Older guests could make the valentines and have them sent to a children's ward in the hospital or perhaps to elderly residents of a rest home.

Bible Hearts

The Bible speaks of many kinds of hearts. Look up the references and find the heart described.

1.	_____ heart	I Kings 3:9	(understanding)
2.	_____ heart	I Kings 3:12	(wise)
3.	_____ heart	Job 23:16	(soft)
4.	_____ heart	Proverbs 25:20	(heavy)
5.	_____ heart	Psalm 119:80	(sound)
6.	_____ heart	Ezekiel 11:19	(stony)
7.	_____ heart	Isaiah 35:4	(fearful)
8.	_____ heart	I Chronicles 12:33	(double)
9.	_____ heart	Isaiah 44:20	(deceived)
10.	_____ heart	Ezekiel 18:31	(new)

Jonathan and His Arrows

Tell the story of Jonathan and the arrows (I Samuel 21: 35ff.). Set up a heart and let the contestants toss arrows or darts at the heart target.

A PATRIOTIC PARTY

I have fought a good fight; I have kept the faith.

PATRIOTIC PARTIES are certainly most appropriate for February. You may plan yours to honor Washington or Lincoln or perhaps just a single patriotic party to honor both of these great men.

Here are some ideas for a Washington party and some for a Lincoln party you may choose from.

INVITATIONS

For a Washington party write your invitations on folded white paper. On the front, decorate with tiny cherries and a hatchet, or tiny flags. Write the main part of your invitation with blue ink, and then with red ink write the place, date, and time of the party.

DECORATIONS AND REFRESHMENTS

Red, white, and blue streamers, bunting, or flags may be used for your decorations. No Washington celebration would be quite complete without the cherry tree, so make this proverbial tree the center of attraction. Select a good shaped branch with many smaller limbs. Spray it with green paint or wrap it with green crepe paper. Bright red gumdrops attached to the branches will make edible "cherries" but do not be surprised if the tree soon looks quite barren. A realistic-looking, but harmless hatchet might lie at the foot of the tree.

A plain white tablecloth will look appropriate. Use strips of red and blue crepe paper to make a border. Or cut out red cherries and green leaves and use those for a colorful border. If you have a red tablecloth, this would look gay with white dishes.

For your centerpiece make a small tree similar to the larger one described. Tiny dolls may be dressed to represent George and Martha Washington.

Place cards may be made from white paper folded in half, with silhouettes of George Washington and his wife placed on front. Or use gummed flags which are very inexpensive. Children would enjoy decorating the place cards with tiny cherry trees.

For individual favors use bright red gumdrops. Cut a slit in the top and insert miniature hatchets cut from heavy paper and colored appropriately.

When you plan your refreshments, you just naturally think of cherry pie. Older guests may prefer cherry pie and coffee while the younger folks usually enjoy cherry pie with ice cream.

Cherry tarts or plain cookies topped with a cherry are appropriate. If you wish to serve sandwiches, make them in patriotic colors by adding food coloring to cream cheese or other fillings. Serve salads which include cherries or cherry-flavored gelatins.

If your party is to be in honor of Lincoln's birthday, you should keep your decorations and refreshments plain and very simple as this seems to be the spirit that dominated the life of this well-loved statesman.

For this type of party why not use your plain old-fashioned red and white or blue and white checked tablecloth. You should also use plain dishes and silverware. For favors use red and white gumdrops alternately with tiny flags stuck in each. Place cards may be made of heavy white paper folded in half with a tiny flag pasted in each corner.

When we think of Lincoln we think of a log cabin, so why not use one for your centerpiece. If the children have building logs, construct a cabin of them. If not, make one from small branches or corrugated paper. Set the cabin in a forest of evergreen sprigs. Build a little rail fence around the cabin. Little colonial people may also be placed about the cabin.

Very simple refreshments should be served. Grownups would like corn bread and beans with a variety of relishes and pickles. Children might not care for such foods. Cookies cut log-shaped or cupcakes decorated with red, white, and blue would be appropriate. Red and white ice cream or plain vanilla ice cream topped with bright red strawberries would carry out the patriotic color scheme.

GAMES

Cutting Down the Cherry Tree

Place a branch in a small container so that it will tip over easily when hit. Give player a piece of wood for a "hatchet." He stands at a designated line, tosses the hatchet at the tree, and scores a point if he succeeds in making the tree fall.

Name It—Red, White, or Blue

Players form a circle and It stands in center. It points to any person in circle and says either "Red," "White," or "Blue." The one to whom he points must name an object of the stated color before It counts to five. If no object is named the two change places. If the person can name an object before five is counted, It must stay in the center.

A Description Game

This may be played orally or as a paper-and-pencil game. Use either the name of George Washington or Abraham Lincoln and ask the players to take each letter separately and write an adjective beginning with each letter to describe that particular president. For example: *G,* generous; *E,* energetic; *O,* obedient; *R,* religious; *G,* great; *E,* expert.

Hunting Games

Children would enjoy hunting for paper hatchets and cherries. For older groups provide a paper flag with the stars missing. Hide small gummed stars about the room and the first to paste 48 stars on his flag is winner.

Do You Know Your Flag?

Show an American flag and then give each person a Bible and the ten references. In each verse, he will find something that is in some way connected with the flag.

Answers:

1. Deuteronomy 25:3 _____ (Stripes)
2. Isaiah 1:18 _____ (White)
3. John 4:35 _____ (Field)
4. Exodus 39:22 _____ (Blue)
5. Isaiah 63:2 _____ (Red)
6. Genesis 37:9 _____ (Stars)
7. Numbers 21:8 _____ (Pole)
8. Jeremiah 48:17 _____ (Staff)
9. Ecclesiastes 4:12 _____ (Cord)
10. Song of Solomon 2:4 _____ (Banner)

A Cherry Race

Use cranberries or small red candies for the "cherries." Place them in a bowl and give each player a knife on which to carry the "cherry." The "cherry" must be taken to a "tree" at the opposite end of the room. If the "cherry" rolls off the knife that player is eliminated. The team with the most "cherries" under the "tree" is winner.

A Good Soldier

Washington was a good soldier. Christians are to be good soldiers for Christ. Find the requirements for a good soldier.

S_____in faith—Romans 4:20   (Strong)
O_____in all things—II Corinthians 2:9   (Obedient)
L_____one another—John 13:34   (Love)
D_____all things through Christ—Philippians 4:13   (Do)
I_____your heart unto the Lord—Joshua 24:23   (Incline)
E_____hardness as a good soldier—II Timothy 2:3   (Endure)
R_____in the Lord—Philippians 3:1   (Rejoice)

This game will be fun for the youngsters, and a hilarious exercise for the older participants. The "Delaware" is a large piece of blue paper placed at the far end of the room. Teams are chosen and the first player takes a small toy boat, races to the "Delaware" (gets on hands and knees) and pushes his boat to the opposite shore. Then he returns to the end of his line. The next player in line races to the "Delaware," bends down, and pushes the boat to the opposite shore. The team which finishes first is declared to be Washington's winning army.

Famous People

Washington and Lincoln are famous men but can you tell what these Biblical persons are known for? Match Column A with the letters in Column B.

A	B		Answers:
1. Naomi	a. Tax collector	————	(1—h)
2. Luke	b. Farmer	————	(2—g)
3. Matthew	c. Well-digger	————	(3—a)
4. Asahel	d. Speed driver	————	(4—e)
5. Paul	e. Foot racer	————	(5—f)
6. Jehu	f. Tentmaker	————	(6—d)
7. Nimrod	g. Doctor	————	(7—n)
8. Tubal-Cain	h. Baby sitter	————	(8—l)
9. Isaac	i. Organist	————	(9—c)
10. Jubal	j. Priest	————	(10—i)
11. Peter	k. Fisherman	————	(11—k)
12. Abel	l. Iron worker	————	(12—b)
13. Noah	m. Silversmith	————	(13—o)
14. Aaron	n. Hunter	————	(14—j)
15. David	o. Ship builder	————	(15—p)
16. Demetrius	p. Shepherd	————	(16—m)

Planting the Cherry Tree

This game is a patriotic version of the old game of Pin the Tail on the Donkey. Draw a large limb of a tree, blindfold the players, and ask them to pin a cluster of cherries on the limb. Or draw a limb on heavy cardboard, place it on the floor, and see who can toss cherries on the limb.

A Patriotic Quiz

You may need a history book for this—or better yet, let the history students help. Write out ten questions concerning pertinent facts in the life of the man you wish to honor. Or write incidents from the life of each and see who can match the man and the event correctly. Be sure to include such important events as the Emancipation Proclamation, Crossing the Delaware, Constitutional Convention, Gettysburg Address, and others equally important.

SPRING FESTIVAL

The flowers appear on the earth.

Doesn't the first daffodil, the first robin, the first really warm, bright spring day make you feel like singing the Song of Solomon?

> For, lo, the winter is past
> The rain is over and gone:
>
> The flowers appear on the earth;
> The time of the singing of the birds is come,
>
> And the voice of the turtle is heard in our land.
> Arise, my fair one, and come away.

Surely such a lovely time calls for a very extra special kind of celebration so let us plan for a Spring Festival.

INVITATIONS

Nothing could be more inspiring than the portion of the Canticles quoted in the lines above so why not use them as part of your invitation? Be sure to add the date and place of the party.

Baskets of spring flowers are always a joy to behold, so make your invitations in the form of a basket. Use a tan-colored paper and cut a double basket with a handle. With brown crayola draw lines to give a woven effect. Then cut bright flowers, paste them on green stems and fill your basket with flowers. Tuck your invitation into your basket of flowers.

DECORATIONS

This is the time of year to bring a bit of the gay outdoors inside so be lavish with your bouquets of pussy willows, wild flowers, wild blossoms, tulips, daffodils—any kind of flower that happens to be available.

As some of the ladies especially enjoy any unique type of flower arrangement, you might have some of the artistic ladies of the neighborhood help you.

Yellow and green seems an ideal color scheme. A low bowl filled with daffodils or yellow tulips could form your center-piece between pale green tapers. Around the bowl scatter some of the artificial grass that is used in Easter baskets. Since spring brings thoughts of new life, have tiny bunnies, chicks, or other figurine animals around the centerpiece.

Tiny corsages will make ideal place cards and favors combined. Wrap the stems in green floral paper or strips of tin foil, add a gay bow, and provide pins so the ladies can look their loveliest while they are being served. Use May baskets for nut cups and be sure these hold green and yellow mints or other candies to carry out the color scheme.

REFRESHMENTS

Make open-faced sandwiches using cream cheese tinted yellow and pale green. Flowers for decorations may be cut from pimento or red mingo peppers with stems of green peppers. Roll sandwiches lily fashion, and hold in place with a piece of toothpick. A tiny strip of yellow cheese will form the center of the flower.

Cupcakes need to be covered with fluffy boiled icing and topped with tinted coconut. Make flowers from yellow gum-drops using small slices to form petals. Strips of green gum-drops may form stem and leaves.

Fill your punch bowl with a lemon-colored beverage. Lemon or orange slices, with "notched" edges floating on top will resemble flowers.

GAMES

Spring Festival

Ask each person to write a word pertaining to spring using

the letters in "Spring Festival." Your list might include such words as:

*S*unshine	*E*aster
*P*lanting	*S*howers
*R*ain	*T*ulips
*I*ris	*I*ndustrious
*N*ests	*V*iolets
*G*ardens	*A*pril
*F*lowers	*L*ove

Spring Bouquet

Give each player the name of a common flower. The one who is It marches around the circle calling out names of flowers. When two are called they must exchange places and It tries to get one of the chairs. The one left standing becomes It.

Naming the Flowers

Find pictures of flowers (or this could be birds), number each and see what person can identify the most correctly within a given time.

Put the Flowers in the Bowl

Place a wooden or nonbreakable bowl in the middle of the room. Each player is given five artificial flowers with small weights on them. Each flower he can toss into the bowl counts five points. This game can also be played by teams if there is a large group.

A Spring Romance

"In the springtime a young man's fancy turns to thoughts of love." Here is the story of a young man. You will need to fill in the blanks with names of flowers to see if there is a happy ending.

"Do you think she will marry me?" _____ (1) _____ said to his mother.

"Why don't you (2) ____," was the wise reply.

So he hurried to the home of beautiful (3) ____ O'Grady. It was just (4) ____ in the afternoon. The (5) ____ were chiming the hour. Our hero rapped loudly on the door.

"____ (6) ____ ____ and see who is knocking," he heard the girl say to her youngest brother.

"It is only Willie," her brother said as he ushered the bashful young man into the room.

"Will you marry me?" stammered the young man, fidgeting with his ____ (7) ____.

"No," she replied.

"But I thought every girl wanted to march down the aisle and wear a ____ (8) ____," he insisted.

"You are poor," she told him haughtily. "When I marry, I shall (9) ____."

"But I can give you everything," he promised with his (10) ____ trembling.

"How can you (11) ____ that?" giggled little brother.

"I shall never marry you!" said the girl angrily, like a snarling ____ (12) ____.

The young man started for the door looking like a shrinking (13) ____.

"I shall never be happy again," he cried. "I shall go home and mourn and perhaps I shall even (14) ____."

ANSWERS

1—Sweet William	6—Johnny-jump-up	11—Lilac
2—Aster	7—Bachelor's button	12—Snap Dragon
3—Rose	8—Bridal wreath	13—Violet
4—Four o'clock	9—Marigold	14—Balsam
5—Bluebells	10—Tulips	

A Scriptural Garden

In the springtime we think of planting. This garden story must have words from the Bible to make it complete. Look up the references and fill in the blanks.

Before we can have a garden we must find some _____ (Luke 8:8). Then we work and _____ (Isaiah 28:24) all day. Next we must break up all the _____ (Hosea 10:11). A hurried trip must be made to the store so we can buy some _____ (Deuteronomy 28:38). Soon we have all of our ground _____ (I Corinthians 3:6).

We must depend upon God in His goodness to send the _____ (Ecclesiastes 11:7) and the _____ (Ecclesiastes 11:3). Even while we are sleeping God will see that the dew ____ ____ (II Samuel 17:12). But we cannot be lazy or our crops will be choked out by the ___ and ___ (Genesis 3:18).

After several weeks we may look across the valleys and see them covered with _____ (Psalm 65:13). We shall thank God, for then we shall know that the ____ ____ ____ (Matthew 9:37).

ANSWERS

Luke 8:8—Good ground
Isaiah 28:24—Plow
Hosea 10:11—Clods
Deuteronomy 28:38—Seed
I Corinthians 3:6—Planted
Ecclesiastes 11:7—Sun
Ecclesiastes 11:3—Rain

II Samuel 17:12—Falleth upon the ground
Genesis 3:18—Thorns
Genesis 3:18—Thistles
Psalm 65:13—Corn
Matthew 9:37—Harvest is plenteous

SPRINGTIME—A TULIP TEA

Perhaps this spring you would like to have something a little different for a springtime party, either for your club or for a church group.

A "Tulip Tea" is a very lovely and easy type of entertainment. There is something about tulips that gladdens our hearts.

INVITATIONS

Make the invitations in the form of tulips. Tuck several of these brightly colored flowers into a vase you have cut from folded paper. Write your invitation details on the backs of these flowers. If your guests are gardeners, ask each one to bring along one of her favorite tulips for display.

DECORATIONS

It is a foregone conclusion that you will have bouquets of tulips for your decorations. When the guests arrive have containers for the flowers. You will find that you have a most colorful display so have a table with a plain white cloth prepared for this tulip exhibit.

ENTERTAINMENT SUGGESTIONS

Naturally you will want to take time for each lady to show her prize flower and perhaps you should have paper and pencil on hand so others might write the name of the particular varieties. Ask each person to tell where the bulbs could be obtained.

It seems likely that you will be able to find some successful gardener in your community who will be willing to speak on the cultivation of tulips. You might be able to obtain special films on tulips or someone could give a demonstration on arrangement of these flowers.

A musical number or two would make a well-rounded program.

Ask each lady to vote for the variety of tulip she likes best. You could give a prize to the lady who brought the favorite flower. A vase, flower holder, and gardening gloves are among suitable prizes.

REFRESHMENTS

Tea and coffee with "tulip" cookies make suitable refreshments. If you do not have a tulip cooky cutter, you can make one easily from a small round tin lid. Bend the top of the lid into three points to resemble a tulip. Cut a long strip of dough for the stem and attach to flower. Add a leaf on each side of the stem. Use green frosting on stems and leaves, and the tulips will be as colorful as your own tulip bed.

A MAYPOLE PARTY

A MAYPOLE PARTY is fun in the springtime and can be made adapted to various age groups. It cannot be surpassed for entertaining youngsters out of doors. Here are some suggestions which you may vary to suit the particular group you are entertaining.

INVITATIONS

Since this is a Maypole party, make your invitations in the form of a miniature Maypole. A plastic drinking straw, cut into about three-inch lengths will form the pole. To the top of the pole glue or staple ribbon streamers about 2½ inches long. On the end of each streamer attach tiny pieces of paper bearing the necessary information concerning the party. This unique invitation wlil slip neatly into an envelope.

DECORATIONS

Here again a Maypole is essential. Very young children would surely enjoy an outdoor Maypole. Perhaps you have a pole in your yard or a small tree which could serve as the Maypole. A clothesline prop anchored in the ground would do. Heavy twine or light rope, braided with crepe paper, will make the Maypole streamers. Children will enjoy singing gay songs as they dance around the Maypole.

A Maypole should also be the center of attraction for an indoor party. A miniature one could very well be your centerpiece. A piece of cane fishing pole, a piece of heavy paper rolled, or even a large candle may form the pole. This should be covered with crepe paper. Anchor the pole on a smooth board or other heavy base. Cover the base with green paper or leaves and place tiny borders of flowers around it. To the top of the pole attach streamers of narrow strips of crepe paper or narrow ribbon. Twist the streamers and run them to each plate. Attach these to place cards or to an inexpensive gift or favor.

An edible Maypole centerpiece is a several-layered cake iced in white and decorated with flowers and green leaves. Through the center of the cake place a small stick about a foot in height. A round stick such as you find on large inflated balloons or small flags would do. Wrap the stick in harmonizing colored paper or ribbon. Attach streamers to the top of the pole and allow them to reach out to the table and be held down with bows, flowers, figurines, or other items in keeping with the type of party you are planning.

Smaller Maypoles for individual favors may be made similarly using cupcakes for the base and stick candy for the poles. Little streamers can be held to the table with packages of gum, bars, or rolls of mints.

GAMES

Any favorite outdoor games will be suitable for this party. Small children will want to play a few games, and then come back to the Maypole.

For an older group, any of the games suggested for the Spring Festival festivities will be appropriate.

MOTHER'S DAY PARTY

THERE ARE USUALLY a number of Mother-Daughter teas and banquets held during the month of May, but perhaps you would like to have a small party just especially for your mother. This could be a small affair with several of the neighbors as guests or a surprise get-together for Mother.

INVITATIONS

Your invitations may be written on plain white stationery with a carnation drawn across the upper lefthand corner. If your party is to be just a family affair, perhaps the children would like to prepare breakfast or dinner and have Mother as their guest. In this case, why not present Mother with a corsage or potted plant and tie a little note to it explaining the plan to her.

DECORATIONS

Mother Nature is very lavish at this time of year, so it will be no trouble to have a bouquet of flowers for a centerpiece. A low bowl filled with pink flowers or blossoms would help carry out the pink and white color scheme. Pink candles too would make the table look more party-like.

For an unusual centerpiece have a "mother pushing a baby carriage," filled with flowers. A pound coffee tin may form the container for the flowers. From very heavy cardboard make the two sides and back and front of the carriage. Paint these and glue them together to fit around the coffee tin. Fill the carriage with flowers and a bit of fernery. Dress a small doll to represent the mother and stand it as if she were pushing the carriage.

To make flower nut cups, cover an ordinary white nut cup with pink crepe paper petals.

For a bit of humor, make place cards with pictures showing a typical "mother's day." Show mother scrubbing, cooking, or doing any of the hundreds of household chores. If you are having guests, make their cards realistic. A mother of a new baby might have a place card showing her walking the floor with a crying child. A mother of several boys might be shown scrubbing a dirty floor, while a mother of several girls would no doubt be shown at an ironing board.

ENTERTAINMENT

You will not need much in the way of entertainment because a group of mothers will spend a pleasant afternoon just visiting. It would be fun, however, to ask each mother to bring along a wedding picture. Daughters might bring along baby pictures. You might give a prize to the one who can identify the most correctly.

Famous Mothers of the Bible

Can you match the mothers in the first column with the children in the second column.

				Answers:
1.	Ruth	a.	Reuben _____	(1—c)
2.	Rebekah	b.	Timothy _____	(2—e)
3.	Eunice	c.	Obed _____	(3—b)
4.	Jochebed	d.	Isaac _____	(4—g)
5.	Rachel	e.	Jacob _____	(5—i)
6.	Elisabeth	f.	Samuel _____	(6—j)
7.	Eve	g.	Moses _____	(7—l)
8.	Sarah	h.	Ishmael _____	(8—d)
9.	Hagar	i.	Joseph _____	(9—h)
10.	Bathsheba	j.	John _____	(10—k)
11.	Leah	k.	Solomon _____	(11—a)
12.	Hannah	l.	Cain _____	(12—f)

How Do You Score as a Mother?

This will be a fun quiz to give the mothers. See who has the highest score.

1. Count 1 point for every child.
2. Count 2 points for every grandchild.
3. Count 10 points for each set of twins in the family.
4. Count 5 points for every child in high school.
5. Count 10 points for every child in college.
6. Count 5 points for every red-headed child in the family.
7. Count 20 points for every married child.
8. Count 20 points if you went to church Sunday with a child or grandchild.
9. Count 10 points if you baked cookies this week.
10. Subtract 10 points if you paddled a child this week.

SUGGESTIONS

If you wish to give some prizes, you might give a prize to the oldest mother present (if the women will divulge their ages), a prize to the newest mother, a prize to the mother with the most children or grandchildren.

Since there are many flowers in our gardens at this time of the year, why not make corsages for prizes. You will find how to make them in a later chapter in this book.

A SUNDAY SCHOOL PICNIC OR
PARTY

Where two or three are gathered together in my name,
there am I in the midst of them.

FOR THE MOST PART, Sunday school picnics are held in parks
where playground equipment and the swimming pool
take care of the entertainment.

However, if you are planning a Sunday school party where
you do not have these facilities or if the weather does not
permit outdoor playing, you will find a well-planned party
necessary to handle a large group.

INVITATIONS

For a Sunday school party, I would suggest either of these
invitations. Small favors may be purchased for a very nominal fee. For example, a pencil with Scripture verse on it
could be given. Tie a little note to the pencil saying, "Use
this pencil to mark June 14 on your calendar so you will not
forget the date of our Sunday school picnic." A ruler might
have a note attached which says, "It is the rule to have a picnic this year. We will meet June 14 at the city park." Or a
bookmark might bear this invitation: "Mark this place in
your book—June 14—Sunday school picnic."

You might make your invitation in the form of a hymn-
book. Make black or dark blue backs and white paper for the
leaves. Tie together with gold-colored thread. Use gold ink
and print "Sunday School Party" on the front.

On the first page print:

O come, let us sing unto the Lord. . . .
Let us come before his presence with thanksgiving
—Psalm 95.

On the second page, print the invitation. And it would be a good idea to suggest each bring his Bible if you plan to have Bible games and references.

Sometimes a Sunday school picnic will include just certain age groups or classes. But quite often the entire church group enjoys a basket dinner and picnic.

Therefore, the following ideas and suggestions you will be able to adapt to your particular group.

Our invitations suggested that we "come and sing unto the Lord." This is a good way to get your group together or to keep the first occupied until the rest arrive. Sing some lively choruses, sing them in rounds, have the boys and girls sing various parts—in short, make the singing a happy occasion.

Biblical A B C

The group may be divided into teams, putting younger and older ones equally on the teams. The first team names a person in the Bible whose name begins with *A*, the next with *B*, and so on until all but one team is eliminated.

Thou Shalt Call His Name

Many names in the Scripture are used when referring to God or Jesus. Beginning with *A* name as many alphabetically as you can. There could be Alpha, Bread of life, Christ, Door, Everlasting, Friend, God, and so on.

Bible-Story Hour

If you have a number of smaller children at a picnic you will find them playing almost too strenuously. Call them in and have a Bible-storytelling hour. Perhaps the minister would give an illustrated lesson. Children enjoy dramatizing stories. Or they could be given paper and crayon and illustrate the story that is told.

A Bible Quiz

1. What had Timothy known from the time he was a small child?—II Timothy 3 _____
2. What two things did a small boy give to Jesus?—John 6 _____
3. What did the child Samuel say when the Lord called him?—I Samuel 3 _____
4. What baby had his bed in a river?—Exodus 2 _____
5. What two wild animals had young David killed?—I Samuel 17 _____
6. What does God want all children to do?—Ephesians 6 _____
7. What would God have you do when you are young? Ecclesiastes 12 _____
8. What does God promise children who obey and honor their parents?—Ephesians 6 _____
9. What animals destroyed the children who mocked Elisha?—II Kings 2 _____
10. What does God say that children have in Heaven? —Matthew 18 _____

ANSWERS

1. The holy Scriptures
2. Five barley loaves and two small fishes
3. "Speak; for thy servant heareth"
4. Moses
5. Lion, bear
6. Obey your parents
7. "Remember thy creator"
8. "Thou mayest live long on the earth"
9. Two she bears
10. Their angels

Women in the Bible

1. What lady had to keep sewing because her child grew so fast from year to year? _____ (Hannah)
2. What woman worried about her housework? _____ (Martha)

3. What woman should win the nail-driving contest? _____ (Jael)
4. What mother-in-law was well liked? _____ (Naomi)
5. What lady met her future husband by working in the field? _____ (Ruth)
6. What woman sewed for others? _____ (Dorcas)
7. What woman was punished for her curiosity? _____ (Lot's wife)
8. What woman is mentioned as being a good grandmother? _____ (Lois)
9. What woman was the first to see the risen Lord? _____ (Mary Magdalene)
10. What woman helped her son deceive her husband? _____ (Rebekah)
11. What woman anointed the feet of Jesus? _____ (Mary)
12. What woman is mentioned as Mary's cousin? _____ (Elisabeth)

Whom Would You Ask?

The boys will enjoy this quiz. Answers are men from the Scriptures.
1. If you wanted to build a boat, whom would you ask for help? _____ (Noah)
2. If you wanted to make a tent? _____ (Paul)
3. If you wanted to catch more fish? _____ (Peter)
4. If you wanted to climb a tricky tree? _____ (Zacchaeus)
5. If you wanted to ride faster? _____ (Jehu)
6. If you wanted to learn to shoot a bow and arrow? _____ (Jonathan)
7. If you wanted to hunt? _____ (Nimrod)
8. If you wanted to build up your muscles? _____ (Samson)
9. If you wanted to hunt big game? _____ (David)
10. If you wanted to train lions? _____ (Daniel)

This game is described under "Miscellaneous Games" and is an ideal game for playing with a large group or with different age groups.

When your picnic finally ends, call all the group together for a parting hymn and a closing prayer.

Each teacher should make sure that every one of the younger children are accounted for before the crowd says good-by.

FOURTH OF JULY—FAMILY STYLE

Ye shall know the truth and the truth shall make you free.

THE FOURTH OF JULY is often a time for family reunions and picnics. So first we shall discuss ideas for a party, family style.

INVITATIONS

Since this is to be a "popping" good affair, start things off with a bang and make invitations in the form of a firecracker. Draw a firecracker on a folded sheet of heavy paper and insert a piece of red, white, and blue thread for the fuse. Write words like these, "Things will start popping when the Dooley clan get together at our house for their annual Fourth of July celebration."

If you prefer to be a bit more realistic, staple a tiny firecracker in the corner of a white correspondence card and print your invitation in red and blue inks.

DECORATIONS

Most people find that the American flag waving a gay welcome is decoration enough. However, you may wish to make your dining room or your patio a bit more festive with bunting or red, white, and blue crepe paper. A white tablecloth should have gummed stars around the edges to form a border.

Make a large firecracker centerpiece by covering cardboard tubes with silver paper and adding bands of red, white, and blue. Tie a gay bow around the center. A white candle may protrude to form the fuse. After the meal is ended, "pop" open the firecracker to reveal candy, balloons, sparklers, or treats for the children.

For place cards, use Tootsie Rolls wrapped in colored paper to resemble a firecracker. Add a piece of pipe cleaner for fuse.

FOOD

The traditional fried chicken, corn on the cob, cole slaw, and ice cream and cake seem to be the accepted menu for the Fourth of July. When you plan a meal for a definite time, serve it at that time. Children should be served first. Paper plates and cups are of definite advantage for this type of meal and allow the children to manage quite well with little assistance from their mothers. If the table is crowded, find a nice shady spot and let the children have a little picnic by themselves.

To avoid "tummy aches" for the children save the ice cream and cake for later in the afternoon.

GAMES

Older folk are very happy just to sit and visit but not so with children. Unless the children are kept entertained, there will be little chance for visiting.

Ask some of the teen-aged boys and girls to help with the small ones. A swing or two put up for the afternoon is a great help. Children may not like taking turns so try this idea. Provide the supervisors with cap guns and when the gun "pops" that child's turn is over. This makes it fun for all.

Nearly every child loves a sandpile, so why not provide some sand, old pans, sieves, and spoons? If the day is warm and the mothers approve, a sprinkler of water will naturally suggest making "pies."

Because children love treasure hunts, it would be well to hide a few small items and let them search. There should be a prize for every child.

Seeing Stars

This is a game for the entire group. Draw a large flag on sheets of paper and give each team 48 stars made of heavy cardboard. The object of the game, of course, is to see which team, in an equal number of tosses can place the most stars in the blue corner of the flag.

Poppety Pop

For a noisy game give each player a balloon to blow up and tie to his wrist. The one whose balloon bursts last is winner of the game. Often children are reluctant to have balloons broken. Inform them that one balloon will have a mystery note inside. This note will tell where there is a Treasure Chest. This will contain anything you think suitable for your group such as fireworks, suckers, or other items.

SUGGESTIONS

There must be time throughout the day for picture taking. And what could be more fun than an impromptu program. The children will have fun planning the "show" and the parents will be an appreciative audience.

In the evening provide some fireworks for the children but do play safe. This must be carefully supervised and parents must keep an eye on the young children.

While the Fourth of July is a grand time for reunions and fireworks, it is well to keep in mind the true meaning of Independence Day. Say "Good-by" by singing "America" and then ask God to continue shedding His love upon "America, the Beautiful."

AN INDEPENDENCE DAY PARTY

A<small>NY DAY IN</small> J<small>ULY</small> is a good day for celebrating the independence of our country. And for such a party, you just could not get away from the traditional red, white, and blue color scheme.

I<small>NVITATIONS</small>

Invitations may be written on folded white paper that has been bordered with gold or various colored gummed stars. You may write the invitation in blue or red ink. Another idea would be to use heavier white paper folded. Cut a slit on the front and insert a tiny American flag.

D<small>ECORATIONS</small>

Naturally Old Glory will be given a prominent place at this party. But you may add a holiday air by using bunting, red, white, and blue crepe paper streamers, or balloons in the three colors. Later these balloons may be used for noise makers.

Bouquets are always nice and at this time of the year, you may be able to find red, white, and blue flowers to arrange artistically. Red and white blossoms will surely be available, and these, in a blue vase, would carry out your patriotic color scheme.

For table decorations use a plain white cloth with a border of stars or crepe paper strips of red and blue to form a border.

There are various appropriate centerpieces which you can make quickly. A floral centerpiece of red, white, and blue flowers could be used. Balloons in the three colors could substitute for flowers. Or a bowl might have small flags in the flower holder. Blue or red candles might be used. The centerpiece might be placed upon a golden star and the candle holders could sit upon smaller star mats. Make these stars from cardboard and gild them.

Each place card could be a piece of folded white paper with a flag stuck through the corner. Nut cups could be in red, white, and blue. Or plain white nut cups with stars attached, and red and blue ribbon bows would add a touch of color.

For a children's party, blow up red, white, and blue balloons, print the child's name on each with nail polish, and attach these to the chairs.

REFRESHMENTS

For whatever type of party, or whatever age group you have invited, you will carry out your patriotic color scheme in your refreshments. Open-faced sandwiches may be cut in the shape of stars. Or half slices of sandwich bread may be decorated like flags using dots of cheese for the stars. Red, white, and blue sandwiches can be made by tinting cream cheese, spreading it between slices of sandwich bread, and cutting them crosswise. Also make those salads and desserts which will carry through the color scheme.

To make a "flag" cake, bake your favorite cake in a large loaf pan. Cover it with smooth white icing, then add red stripes and the blue field. Add yellow stars in the corner. This idea could be used for cookies too.

GAMES

Red, White, or Blue?

The person who is It stands in the center of a circle. He points to a player, says either "red," "white," or "blue." The person to whom he has pointed must name an object of that color before It counts five. For example if the color designated were red, the person might reply "tomato." White could be snow, and blue could be sky.

A Bible Quiz

Take the first of every word
Place them in a row;
You will find a special day,
One you love, I know.

1. The son of Abraham and Sarah. _____ (Isaac)
2. Builder of an ark. _____ (Noah)
3. Put into the lions' den. _____ (Daniel)
4. Was taken up into Heaven. _____ (Elijah)
5. Was saved on the Damascus Road. ____ (Paul)
6. A famous queen. _____ (Esther)
7. A king who had a dream. _____ (Nebuchad-
   nezzar)
8. Sweet psalmist. _____ (David)
9. Means going out. _____ (Exodus)
10. Cured of leprosy. _____ (Naaman)
11. He slew his brother. _____ (Cain)
12. Had a vision of dry bones. _____ (Ezekiel)

What Am I?

Below are a list of familiar things which may be described with a color—red, white, or blue.

1. An elephant no one wants. _____ (White)
2. You may see this color when angry. _____ (Red)
3. The Israelites crossed this sea. _____ (Red)
4. Grass in Kentucky. _____ (Blue)
5. Famous football Grange. _____ (Red)
6. A surrendering flag. _____ (White)
7. A ridge of mountains in Virginia. _____ (Blue)
8. A favorite Christmas. _____ (White)
9. Mondays. _____ (Blue)
10. Mountains in the East. _____ (White)

The Liberty Bell Rings Again

Tie a small bell in a doorway. Give each player or team

a tennis ball and see who can ring the bell the most times in a certain number of throws.

A Sing Down

Choose up teams and have one team sing the first line of "America," the second team the next line and on through the song. When one teams fails to sing the line correctly, it is eliminated. Other patriotic songs may be used.

Matching the Heroes

Some famous characters in American history and some in the Bible are known for similar deeds. Can you match them? Column 1 contains the heroic or well-known deed, column A the historical character, and column B the Biblical character.

Column 1	A	B
1. Levying taxes	a. Paul Revere	I. Aaron _____
2. Crossing a body of water	b. Cornwallis	II. Jonah _____
3. Orator	c. Arnold	III. Goliath _____
4. Traitor	d. Hale	IV. Caleb _____
5. Seamstress	e. King George	V. Augustus Caesar _____
6. Symbol of freedom	f. Bill of Rights	VI. Command-ments _____
7. Famous for "10"	g. Webster	VII. Serpent on Pole _____
8. Warning of danger	h. Liberty Bell	VIII. Judas _____
9. Spied out land	i. Washington	IX. Israelites _____
10. Had to surrender	j. Betsy Ross	X. Dorcas _____

ANSWERS

1—e—V	3—g—I	5—j—X	7—f—VI	9—d—IV
2—i—IX	4—c—VIII	6—h—VII	8—a—II	10—b—III

How Well Do You Know Your History Lesson?

Place on a table ten groups of objects which are symbolic of something famous in American history. Pass out paper and pencils to write down answers.

1. Picture of a Plymouth car and a rock. (Plymouth Rock)
2. Some tea and thumb tacks. (The tea tax)
3. A clock with a minute hand and a toy gun. (Minute men)
4. Piece of hickory stick. (Old Hickory—Andrew Jackson)
5. Small log and ax. (Lincoln, the Rail-splitter)
6. A kite and key. (Franklin, discoverer of electricity)
7. Picture of refrigerator with 1867 printed on it. (Purchase of Alaska, laughingly called, "Seward's ice box")
8. Picture of a valley and a small forge. (Valley Forge)
9. Toy railroad covered with black cloth. (Underground railroad)
10. Tiny sieve and something to resemble gold. (Gold rush)
11. A tea ball in a fancy cup. (Boston tea party)
12. A white flower and a compact. (Mayflower compact)

A RAINBOW PARTY FOR SUMMER

I do set my bow in the cloud.

IN THE SUMMER TIME there is nothing lovelier to behold
than a rainbow. And a Rainbow party is equally exciting
and beautiful. For the younger folk, we can make the party
more exciting. For adults, the rainbow theme can be carried
out in a colorful mood.

INVITATIONS

For our invitations we color a brilliant rainbow across
the front of a folded sheet of white stationery. At the foot of
the rainbow, we must put a pot of gold. Inside write these
lines:

> There's a little fortune waiting—
>   Or so we're often told;
> So come and we shall search for it
>   Within that pot of gold.

DECORATIONS

Often in the summer an outdoor party is enjoyed. At any
rate, you will need a rainbow. This can be fashioned either
inside or outdoors with some fine wire and bright-colored
crepe paper. At the foot of the rainbow have a black kettle
filled with gold. This gold may be prizes wrapped in gold
foil.

Progressive games would be fun for this occasion and you
could set up several small utility tables even on the lawn.
Cover the tables with bright cloths to look like rainbow
colors. In the center of each place a very low bowl of yellow flowers. Or you might place a small bowl of yellow can-

dies to munch while playing games. Provide a variety of games. At one table there might be checkers, at another Chinese checkers—any that your guests would enjoy. The person who wins at the first table moves to the second table; the one at the second table moves up one place. The winners finally end at a table where a pot of gold holds a prize for them.

Children might tire of progressive games so here are a few more boisterous ideas.

The Pot of Gold

Choose up relay teams. The first player on each team is given a gold-covered coin and at a signal he takes the coin, runs to the rainbow, then comes back and gives the coin to the next player on his team. This continues down the line and the first team through is winner.

Chasing Rainbows

Mark two bases with bright-colored paper and designate these as "Rainbows." The person who is It stands in the center and holds a "piece of gold." When he calls out, "Chasing rainbows," the players must leave the base on which they are standing and run to the other rainbow base. If the person who is It tags a runner with the gold coin, that person must be It too. Continue until all players are caught.

Noah and the Ark

Acquaint the players with the story of the first rainbow following the Flood. The person who is It is Noah. All of the players are given names of animals. They stand on a base and Noah calls out the names of animals. When the player hears his "animal name" called, he tries to run safely to a base called the Ark. If he is caught before he reaches the safety of the Ark, he must help Noah catch the other animals.

Rainbow Fortunes

When the games are completed, you may tell **Rainbow Fortunes**. Each player draws out a piece of colored paper. Provide enough colors so every one of the players will have a color. As each person holds up the rainbow color he drew, you will read his fortunes as follows.

Rainbow Fortunes

You were lucky when you chose red:
You'll have adventure before going to bed.

You picked a lovely shade of blue:
That means great riches will come to you.

Yours is yellow, the color of gold;
You'll have great wealth—when you are old.

Purple is a royal hue;
Soon a throne will be for you.

Green's the color of money—true—
It means the "grass to mow"—for you.

Orange color is a lucky one;
You'll not have wealth, but you'll have fun.

Pink is such a color gay;
You'll make friends just every day.

Gold in the Bible

Many times gold is mentioned in the Bible. Can you find these:

1. Pharaoh put a gold _____ about his neck. Genesis 41:42
2. Neither shall ye make unto you _____ of gold. Exodus 20:23
3. They laid the ark of the Lord upon the cart of the coffer with the _____ of gold. I Samuel 6:11
4. As a _____ of gold in a swine's snout. Proverbs 11:22

5. The image's _____ was of fine gold. Daniel 2:32
6. A man with a gold _____. James 2:2
7. The building of the wall of it was of jasper and the _____ was pure gold. Revelation 21:18
8. Aaron said unto them, "Break off the golden _____." Exodus 32:2
9. The _____ of the city was pure gold. Revelation 21:21
10. A word fitly spoken is like _____ of gold. Proverbs 25:11

ANSWERS

1. Chain	3. Mice	5. Head	7. City	9. Street
2. **Gods**	4. Jewel	6. Ring	8. Earrings	10. Apples

God's Rainbow

Remind the younger ones of the Flood and the bow God set in the clouds.

1. What were the names of Noah's sons? _____ (Shem, Ham, Japheth)
2. How long did Noah warn the people of the coming danger? _____ (120 years)
3. How many people went into the ark? _____ (8)
4. How many days and nights did it rain? _____ (40)
5. Where did the ark come to rest? _____ (Mount Ararat)
6. What bird did Noah turn loose first? (Raven)
7. What did the dove bring back? _____ (Olive leaf)
8. Who shut the door of the ark? _____ (God)
9. What did Noah do as soon as he came out of the ark? _____ (Built an altar unto the Lord)
10. What does God promise when we see a rainbow? _____ (Never again shall a flood destroy the entire earth)

Finding the Treasure at the End of the Rainbow

Before the guests arrive have these notes hidden. The last note may bring them to a table set beneath a rainbow. Or outdoors the note may lead to a picnic table with refresh-

60

ments. As the guests knock at the door, the last note suggests you present them with a pot of gold-wrapped favors and then lead them to the "eats."

Give them this note first. Each is written on colored "rainbows."

1. Go real fast,
    Look at the gate.
   Get the note—
    Do not wait.

2. On the front porch,
    Stop and look,
   There is a note
    Under a book.

3. The gold's not here,
    But go to a tree.
   Find a big rock
    Pick up what you see.

4. Now find a big kettle,
    It is in plain sight;
   There is a clue
    That'll lead you aright.

5. Go back to the house—
    To the kitchen door—
   Knock only three times,
    Not less! Not more!

(These directions may be simplified or made harder according to the group you are entertaining.)

Give the treasure seekers their pot of gold with balloons or other favors in it and now it is time to eat.

REFRESHMENTS

If the party is outdoors, the guests will enjoy plain picnic food. A meat loaf may be served that will carry out the Treasure theme if you place hard boiled eggs in the center as you shape it. When this is cut into servings, the egg makes the golden color through the center.

Tiny round cookies, frosted in yellow, carry out the coin theme. Candies or popcorn balls may be wrapped in yellow cellophane or gold foil paper.

Remember that in a Rainbow party, *color* is necessary. So make this as cheery as the sunshine and rainbow after a summer shower.

AN A B C PARTY FOR SCHOOL DAYS

Wisdom is the principal thing.

DURING THE SCHOOL YEAR you may want to have a party for no particular reason other than having your friends together for a jolly evening.

What would be more appropriate than an A B C party?

INVITATIONS

Make your invitations in the form of a report card—*if* you think it won't frighten the gang away.

> I'm going to have *A* party.
> You   *B* sure to come.
> I want to   *C* you there—
> At eight begins the fun.

REFRESHMENTS AND SUGGESTIONS

No need to do a lot of preparing for this party. It would even be fun to take them to the kitchen, provide ice cream, and let them take over from there—malts, root beer floats, sundaes. Or bring out the bread and let them do a "Dagwood" sandwich. How about making taffy, popping corn, or stirring up a batch of fudge?

Just be sure that you leave the kitchen clean for Mother when she comes down to get breakfast next morning.

GAMES

Probably you have some favorite games so set up small utility tables and let them choose what they wish. You may have some new records that are waiting to be played or some new sheet music that is fun to try harmonizing.

If Father is trying to get some sleep, you had better try some of the quieter games later in the evening.

What Lessons Do You Prefer?

Do you even know what lessons you study in school? Here they are—you tell me.

1. Per gay hog   ————————— (Geography)
2. Hit time car   ————————— (Arithmetic)
3. Sell Ping   ————————— (Spelling)
4. U lea gang   ————————— (Language)
5. Ade Ring   ————————— (Reading)
6. The hal   ————————— (Health)
7. Since E C   ————————— (Science)
8. Win grit   ————————— (Writing)
9. Hams tame tic   ————————— (Mathematics)
10. I C Sum   ————————— (Music)

Choosing Partners

If you wish to choose partners for a game have the boys toss one of their shoes in a pile. The girl's partner "must fit the shoe." Or you may do this vice versa and let the boy select the girl's slipper.

Do You Know Your Geography?

Give each player the outline of the 48 states, each state drawn separately. The one who can identify the most correctly by their shape is winner.

Capitals and States

This may be played with many variations. If you wish to choose partners, let the boys draw the state and the girls the capitals. Match state and capital for partner.

Choose teams and when one side names a capital the other must name the state or if a player names the state, his opponent must name the state capital.

Identify These

Unscramble Column A and match correctly with Column B.

A	B	
1. Ham jaalt	a. China	_____
2. Herin	b. India	_____
3. Gin ebb	c. Italy	_____
4. Ike npg	d. India	_____
5. Ea sngg	e. England	_____
6. Liner mk	f. Spain	_____
7. His pxn	g. Germany	_____
8. Abraham L	h. Egypt	_____
9. Pia pan	i. Russia	_____
10. Lamalorb Tealcs	j. England	_____
11. Rat hen nop	k. So. Dakota	_____
12. Ladlyclipic Ruscic	l. Scotland	_____
13. Veirpro	m. Greece	_____
14. Ripd marys	n. Italy	_____
15. Otrdftras Voanon	o. Norway	_____
16. Zider ezue	p. Egypt	_____
17. Isrodf	q. Arizona	_____
18. Darng Oncayn	r. California	_____
19. Otmun Serohumr	s. England	_____
20. Stoktn Rybre Amfr	t. Netherlands	_____

Answers

1. Taj Mahal	d. India
2. Rhine	g. Germany
3. Big Ben	e. England
4. Peking	a. China
5. Ganges	b. India
6. Kremlin	i. Russia
7. Sphinx	h. Egypt
8. Alhambra	f. Spain
9. Appian	c. Italy
10. Balmoral Castle	l. Scotland
11. Parthenon	m. Greece
12. Piccadilly Circus	j. England

13. Po River	n. Italy
14. Pyramids	p. Egypt
15. Stratford-on-Avon	s. England
16. Zuider Zee	t. Netherlands
17. Fiords	o. Norway
18. Grand Canyon	q. Arizona
19. Mount Rushmore	k. So. Dak.
20. Knotts Berry Farm	r. California

An A B C Bible Quiz

The important word omitted in each sentence begins with either *A*, *B*, or *C*.

1. "_____ unto me, all ye that labor." Matthew 11:28
2. "_____ in me, and I in you." John 15:4
3. "_____ on the Lord Jesus Christ, and thou shalt be saved." Acts 16:31
4. "_____ in me a clean heart." Psalm 51:10
5. "_____ thy _____ upon the waters." Ecclesiastes 11:1
6. "_____ things work together for good to them that love God." Romans 8:28
7. "_____ died for the ungodly." Romans 5:6
8. "Ye are _____ with a price." I Corinthians 6:20
9. "Now _____ faith, hope, and _____." I Corinthians 13:13
10. "Christ hath redeemed us from the _____ of the law." Galatians 3:13
11. "_____ we like sheep have gone _____." Isaiah 53:6
12. "_____ not deceived." Galatians 6:7
13. "God forbid that I should glory, save in the _____." Galatians 6:14
14. "_____ _____ with such things as ye have." Hebrews 13:5

ANSWERS

1. Come	6. All	11. All; astray
2. Abide	7. Christ	12. Be
3. Believe	8. Bought	13. Cross
4. Create	9. Abideth; Charity	14. Be content
5. Cast; bread	10. Curse	

Alphabet in Reverse

Get a watch with a large second hand and clock each contestant to see who can say the alphabet backward in the shortest time.

A B C Names

The person who is It points to a player and says either *A, B,* or *C.* Before he counts five that person must give a proper name beginning with the designated letter. You may use person's names, names of cities, or names of Biblical characters.

A HOBO PARTY FOR FALL

COOL, CRISP, STARLIGHT NIGHTS are ideal for a last outdoor party of the season. And what could be more fun than a Hobo Party? You might like to have a hayride or a treasure hunt first.

There will be nothing fancy about any of this party.

INVITATIONS

Write your invitations in pencil on brown wrapping paper or on a heavy brown sack.

> We're hitting the road
>   And want you to go;
> Put on your old clothes
>   Like a real Hobo.
> So come to our house
>   Please use the back gate.
> We're leaving at seven—
>   So don't be late.

Decorations and Games

If you take the gang on a treasure hunt or for a hayride first, bring them back to Hobo's Hideout. If you can use a recreation room or an old garage, use old logs, kegs, boxes, or bundles of straw for seats. Hang old gunny sacks or burlap over the windows. Put up signs saying, "No trespassing," "Beware of Cross Dogs," "Tramps move on," and others.

You might divide your group into teams and send them out searching for a definite list of items. This might include a coffee can, an old bone, a safety pin, some string, a chicken

feather, pencils, beans, cooky, and other objects. The first
team to bring a complete list is victorious.

Feeding the Hobo

Choose partners and blindfold each couple. Give one a
spoon and the other a tin cup of candy corn. The one with
the spoon must feed his partner. The couple emptying the
cup first wins.

Mean Dog, Beware!

A blindfolded Hobo stands in the middle of the circle and
points to a player. The "cross dog" must bark three times.
If the tramp identifies him, they exchange places.

Hold Out the Tin Cup

Set a tin cup in the center of the floor. Give each Hobo
five pennies and see how many he can toss into the cup.

Hitting the Road

The first player says, "I'm hitting the road for _____,"
and he names a city beginning with the letter *A*. The second
player repeats this and adds a city beginning with *B*. When
a player fails to name the cities correctly, he is eliminated
from the game.

The Cops Are Coming

Play this like Black Man, only the player in the center calls
out "The cops are coming" and everyone must run. When
a player is caught, he helps catch the others.

Getting a Handout

A Hobo must be good at getting a handout. Give each a
small paper sack and send him searching about the room for
small articles of food to put in the sack. There might be
grains of rice, beans, candy, corn, peas, chocolate bits, peanuts, nuts, small onions, potatoes. When the whistle blows
the one with the most food is winner.

The Hobo Travels

A hobo travels across the country into many different places. Can you find them? These are all mentioned in I Chronicles.

1. I Chronicles 29:1 _____ (Palace)
2. I Chronicles 6:64 _____ (Suburbs)
3. I Chronicles 15:1 _____ (Tent)
4. I Chronicles 6:56 _____ (Villages)
5. I Chronicles 15:1 _____ (City)
6. I Chronicles 6:66 _____ (Coasts)
7. I Chronicles 19:9 _____ (In a field)
8. I Chronicles 7:28 _____ (Towns)
9. I Chronicles 11:7 _____ (Castle)
10. I Chronicles 12:15 _____ (Valleys)

An Easy Handout

This game may be played by couples, by teams, or individually. Give each person a group of old magazines and some scissors. Prepare a list of foods that a hobo might get in a handout. Find pictures to illustrate. Your list might include a peanut butter sandwich, potato, pie, cake, cup of coffee, bowl of soup, bread and butter, cup of tea, beans, bacon, and so on. See who can get his "handout" first.

Hopping the Freight Train

Play this like musical chairs. Have one less chair than players so when the music stops, one person has "missed the train" and must discontinue his journey. Remove a chair every time someone is out.

REFRESHMENTS

If you can have an outdoor fire or an indoor fireplace, provide wieners, buns, and marshmallows. Line the guests up and give each one a sack with his lunch in it. Serve coffee, hot chocolate, or cold drinks in tin cups or tin cans. Nothing fancy, please.

While the hoboes sit around the fire, roasting marshmallows you will enjoy spinning yarns or loudly singing songs of the road.

PRIZES

If you give any prizes, give bandannas, a folding drinking cup, box of food mix, or other humorous gifts.

When the party is over, blow the whistle and warn your guests that the freight train is pulling out and they had better get aboard.

A HALLOWEEN PARTY—THE CAT'S MEOW!

Let them shout for joy and be glad

I THINK A HALLOWEEN PARTY is one of the very jolliest and one that is remembered longest. There is something about the mysterious, about ghosts and witches, about masquerading, which appeals to all ages.

But before you begin your actual planning, I would like to make one suggestion if you are entertaining young children. There will be a certain element of surprise but do not actually frighten a child. I recall when our four-year-old daughter purchased a witch's mask and then asked me to put it on. I started toward her, but she backed off exclaiming, "I *know* you are my mother but don't come any closer!"

So do let's have a pleasant evening but no nightmares, please!

INVITATIONS

Black cats are the accepted symbols for Halloween, so cut out a black cat and add features and whiskers. If you have some luminous paint use it for features so they will glow in the dark. Your invitations might say:

> Meow! Meow! Meow!
> The cats are prowling tonight;
> If one should cross your lonely path,
> Say quickly and softly, "Star light."
>
> Do not be easily frightened,
> Everything's all right—
> If you come masked to my house
> At seven on Halloween night.
>
> MEOW! MEOW! MEOW!

DECORATIONS

When planning your decorations you cannot do much to improve upon the traditional cornstalks, jack-o'-lanterns, and autumn leaves. If weather permits, an outdoor party is an easy way to entertain. If this is not feasible, a garage, an attic, basement, or vacant building might be used. You can have cornstalks stacked about and lighted jack-o'-lanterns too. Be very cautious if you have candles in the pumpkins. Cut out large black cats and place them in the tree limbs or atop the cornstalks. Use luminous paint for features so they will glow in the light of the bonfire.

If you wish to get a great big "Meow" out of your guests, hide a large ghost in a nearby tree. Paint the ghost's features with luminous paint. When a ghost story is becoming alarming, flash a light in the tree. I doubt that even the blackest swiftest Halloween cat could outrun some of your more timid guests.

If your party is indoors, you might arrange cornstalks and pumpkins around the room. Autumn leaves make artistic arrangements. Pin black cats on the curtains; hang them from the lights and in other prominent places.

GAMES

Masquerading

A Grand March is always fun at a masquerade. Tell your guests, when they arrive, they are to remove their masks when identified. For those hard to guess, they are instructed to answer all questions but only with a "Meow" for an affirmative answer and "Psssssst" for a negative.

The Cat's Meow

Choose up at least three teams. One is the "Cats" and they meow. One is the "Owls" and they hoot. The "Ghosts" moan loudly. Numerous black cats are hidden about the room and everyone is to search for them. However, only the captain of the team is allowed to pick up a cat. When a player finds a cat, he will either meow, hoot, or moan until a captain picks up the cat. This is not a quiet game!

Who Has the Cat? (Action game)

Each player is given the body of a cat. The missing legs, tail, eyes, and ears are hidden. At a given signal the players hunt for the missing parts. The first one to assemble a complete cat is the winner.

Who Has the Cat? (Sitting game)

Before the guests arrive prepare envelopes for each player. Then cut out enough complete cats for each but divide the bodies, legs, tails, eyes, ears and heads. Mix these parts all up so that no envelope has a complete cat. Perhaps one will have ten legs and six eyes. Or it may have all bodies and only an ear. At a given signal, the players begin to trade parts trying to get a complete cat. Do not allow too much time to elapse before calling a halt. Each person is to assemble his cats. The one with the most completed cats is winner.

Black Cat Games for Younger Children

Give each child a paper sack large enough to fit over his head; provide crayons and let each make a black cat mask. They will enjoy "modeling" these.

Children will enjoy pinning the tail on the black cat. They will also enjoy playing "Hide the Thimble" only they hide a black cat and call it "Hiding the Halloween Kitty."

Place a milk bottle on the floor behind a straight-backed chair. The children kneel on the chair, lean over the back, and see how many of their five candy cats they can drop into the bottle.

Place a pumpkin in the center of the room and let the children toss candy cats to the hungry jack-o'-lantern.

The Cat Will Tell Your Fortune

Cut out parts of a cat and place them in a pumpkin. Let

each one draw and then show what part he has drawn. Then read the fortunes.

1. Eyes that are shining
     Big and bright;
   Means you'll see
     Your mate tonight.

2. Ears that are long
     And pointed too;
   Means good news
     Will come to you.

3. Claws that are as sharp
     As the edge of a knife;
   Describes the tongue of
     Your future wife.

4. A long black tail
     Points away up high;
   Shows you will go
     For a ride in the sky.

5. Did you get the whiskers
     So long and so black?
   Watch for a tall man
     Behind your broad back.

6. Here is a foot
     That can't be heard;
   You'll have good fortune
     Just mark this short word.

7. Long black legs
     That jump very far;
   Means you'll be next
     To reach the first star.

Black as a Halloween Cat

The Bible mentions the color black or night many times. How many of these do you know?

1. "Thou canst not make one _____ white or black." (Hair)

2. "Wandering _____, to whom is reserved the blackness of darkness forever." (Stars)
3. "And I beheld, and lo a black _____." (Horse)
4. "There was darkness over all the earth until the _____ hour." (Ninth)
5. "There was a man of the Pharisees, named _____ . . . the same came to Jesus by night." (Nicodemus)
6. "He took not away the pillar of the cloud by day, nor the pillar of _____ by night." (Fire)
7. "It came to pass, that at midnight the Lord smote all the _____ _____ in the land of Egypt. (First-born)
8. "Darkness over the land of Egypt, even darkness which may be _____." (Felt)
9. "The earth was without form, and void; and darkness was upon the _____ of the _____." (Face of the deep)

There's a Cat in the Answer

1. A flood _____ (Cataclysm)
2. Burial place _____ (Catacomb)
3. A large indexed book _____ (Catalog)
4. Wild cat _____ (Catamount)
5. A way to hurl an object _____ (Catapult)
6. Waterfall _____ (Cataract)
7. Bad cold _____ (Catarrh)
8. Calamity _____ (Catastrophe)
9. Shows disapproval _____ (Catcalls)
10. To grasp _____ (Catch)
11. Sauce _____ (Catsup)
12. Form of instruction _____ (Catechism)
13. System or class _____ (Category)
14. Livestock _____ (Cattle)
15. A plant _____ (Catnip)
16. Church _____ (Cathedral)

Telling Fortunes

See the numerous ways to tell fortunes and choose the one most appropriate for your group.

Refreshments

If you have an outdoor party, you will naturally plan to have a bonfire. Wieners, hamburgers, buns, marshmallows are as necessary as the black cats.

Gingerbread and whipped cream are always a favorite too. Cut the gingerbread in round pieces and then make a cat's face on each piece. Whipped cream may outline the features, use candy corn for eyes, and coconut sprinkled in the whipped-cream whiskers will add a realistic touch.

You might cover a square piece of gingerbread with whipped cream, and stand a candy cat on top.

Popcorn ball cats are easy to prepare. The popcorn ball is the cat's head, his ears are orange slices, his features are black jelly beans and his whiskers are pieces of colored drinking straws.

Decorate cookies or cupcakes with chocolate frosting and outline an orange cat on top or vice versa.

A HALLOWEEN PARTY—A WANDERING WITCH PARTY

A WANDERING WITCH PARTY has many possibilities and variations. You might invite the guests to a "Witches' Meeting."

INVITATIONS

For this party, cut out a black broomstick and paste a black witch on the handle. Attach this invitation:

> The witches are flying through the air;
> So grab your broomstick and join them there;
> Ride to my house, don't be late;
> Let the cauldron reveal your fate!

DECORATIONS

A deserted barn, garage, attic, or basement would be a fine hideout for the witches. Or a shady spot in your yard may be prepared with a witch's cauldron over a glowing fire.

This cauldron should be a very conspicuous part of your decorations. You will probably be able to find a black iron kettle or an old kettle which you can paint black. This could hang on a tripod over a fire which you will later use for roasting wieners. Even with an indoor party, you *must* have a cauldron. Pile some small sticks of wood over some red cellophane to represent a fire. If you use a flashlight or a light bulb to give a burning effect, be very careful or it may become *too* realistic.

Either you should dress up as a witch to greet your guests or you may make a witch to stand at the gate and greet them. To make such a witch, use crossed boards such as you would use in fashioning a scarecrow. Drape this figure in loose black clothing and perch a tall black hat on top of her head. A witch's mask will complete the "reception committee."

GAMES

Stunt

For an amusing stunt instruct them all to come as witches and bring a broomstick since they are going to sail around the town. You might divide the group into teams and tell them they are to search the town for ingredients for the witches' stew. Give them a list of things they must bring back. They could be sent out to find such things as a potato, onion, a wooden spoon, some black thread—any such items. You might arrange with some of your friends beforehand to do this trick: tell the witches they are to search for the missing black cat which used to ride on their broomsticks. Send them to a certain house to pick up a box containing the cat's tail. Go to another house and get the cat's head, and so forth. They are warned not to open the box until they return with all of the parts. When they finally come and open the boxes, they find balloons, candy, or various treats.

Where Is the Witch's Broom?

Hide toothpicks which are the straws from the witch's broom. Hide a few colored picks and allow more points for the various colored "straws."

The Witch Has Returned

Select a dark corner for this game and have all the players sit on the floor or the ground and put their hands under a sheet. As you tell this story in weird tones, the various parts of the witch are passed around. Anyone who makes a sound will be required to do some stunt when the story ends.

Many years ago a rich lady lived in the edge of the forest in a large castle. One day a wandering child lost her way and went to the castle to beg for food.

"Get away, you dirty, wretched child!" cried the heartless woman.

A kind fairy overheard the cries of the child as the woman turned her away. The fairy waved her wand and exclaimed, "You selfish woman! You shall become a witch without a place to rest your weary head. You must roam about. On Halloween you shall return to earth and beg for your earthly body."

So tonight the witch has come to find her hand. (Pass a rubber glove filled with wet sand.)

"Please give me my hands so I may knock at your door."

But nobody will give the witch her hands so she slips up and whispers in your ear, "Please give me just one finger, just one finger." (Pass a small sausage around the circle.)

"My ears are missing. Please give me back my ears so I can hear if you ask me to enter your home." (Pass two apricots which are barely cooked.)

"My eyes are gone. I cannot see you! My eyes, please." (Pass two grapes with skins removed.)

"My teeth are gone, alas! I can only sip the magic potion from my magic cauldron. Please return my teeth so I may eat with you tonight." (Pass corn.)

"I am only a spirit from the world of ghosts. My brains are gone. If only you will return my brains." (Pass a small bowl filled with cooked spaghetti.)

"You are not willing to help me? I think I shall come and haunt you. I am a spirit hovering over you. Long ago my earthly body returned to the dust. My blood has long ago clotted and left my lifeless veins. Give me my blood, please." (Pass a bowl of very firm gelatin.)

All of this must be said in a deep sepulchral voice. It would be better if you could persuade someone unknown to the group to speak the lines. (Do not play this with small children.)

Fortunes from the Witch's Cauldron

Have a good talker to act as your witch fortuneteller. Inside the cauldron place an incense burner. This perfumed smoke adds an air of mystery. The fortunes will be even more mysterious if you write the fortunes with lemon juice, roll the paper up tightly, and place in a capsule which you may purchase from any drugstore. When the guests draw out a capsule and remove the paper nothing will be seen until they hold it over the magic fire. A candle flame is ideal for this too. When the lemon juice is held over a low flame, the juice will scorch slightly and the writing becomes visible.

Guess the Witch

Hang a sheet and place a bright light behind it. Have the boys' shadows appear on the sheet. Each boy will wear a witch's hat. Let the girls guess the boys. Then have the girls line up and the boys guess them. This would be a good way to choose partners.

REFRESHMENTS

Your outdoor fire or indoor fireplace will become the "witches' magic fire." Each person gets a broomstick for roasting wieners or marshmallows. These roasting forks are pointed sticks. Wieners are "witches' fingers," and marshmallows are "witches' teeth." Doughnuts are "witches' rings," and the drink will be the "witches' brew." The "witches' heads" are popcorn balls with features made of black jelly beans, and tall pointed hats made of black construction paper and fastened to the top of the popcorn head. Doughnuts may be served off a broom handle.

Have someone call out these various refreshments, and as they are named, the guests come forward to accept them.

If you wish to serve Halloween candies or small favors, serve them in individual witch's hats. To make these cut a circle of black paper for the brim of the hat. A pointed ice-cream cone may be the crown. Fill the crown with candies or noisemakers, then staple to the brim. You may paste a tiny broomstick on the hat, with a person's name on it.

For an edible witch's hat make the brim of a chocolate-covered doughnut. Fill a chocolate cone with ice cream and turn upside down on the doughnut brim.

A HALLOWEEN PARTY

Solve the Puzzle

Found in *Herod* but not in *king;*	(H)
Found in *Asa* but not in *sing.*	(A)
Found in *Lazarus* but not in *ark,*	(L)
Found in *Luke* but not in *Mark;*	(L)
Found in *obey* but not in *bay;*	(O)
Found in *white* but not in *gray;*	(W)
Found in *every* but not in *all,*	(E)
Found in *Elisha* but not in *hall.*	(E)
Found in *Noah* but not in *me;*	(N)

Take the first letters and a word you'll see.

A Halloween Sentence

Have each person try to write a sentence using words beginning with the letters *H, A, L, L, O, W, E, E, N.* You might write something silly like "Have all long, lean, old witches enter every nook."

A Witch's Spelling Contest

Pronounce easy words to the individuals or teams. Only no one is to say the letter *A.* Instead he says, "Broomstick." For example, the word *cat* would be spelled, *C, broomstick, t.* When one misspells, he must drop out of the game. No one is given a second chance.

Describing the Old Witch

The first player says, "The Old Witch is an—," and he supplies an adjective beginning with *A.* The next player repeats the first adjective and adds one beginning with *B*. The sentence might soon sound like this: The Old Witch is an audacious, bad, catty, dirty, elegant, furious, gaunt, hateful—and so on. If one person cannot continue, allow the next player to proceed.

SUGGESTIONS FOR TELLING FORTUNES

Gypsy Fortuneteller

Usually you can find one person who is clever enough to masquerade as a gypsy and tell fortunes. Prepare a darkened corner, a gaily covered table, and a crystal bowl. A rose bowl with a black cat inside would make an appropriate crystal bowl. The fortuneteller's identity should be kept secret and the person should know the group well enough to make the fortunes sound amusing and realistic.

Pumpkin-Seed Fortunes

Collect a number of seeds and color each one differently. The person's future is determined by the color of the seed he draws out of the jack-o'-lantern. Purple stands for royalty and indicates that person will some day hold a position of great influence. Silver means untold wealth. Yellow indicates the person will have a sunny, happy life. Green foretells a life as a farmer. Blue means that person will pioneer space travel. White indicates a life as a doctor or nurse. Black would indicate the life of a hobo.

Your Fortune Is in the Bag

In a heavy cloth bag place a variety of objects which will indicate the person's fortune. If a player draws out a ruler this means he will become a teacher; knife foretells a medical career; badge indicates an officer of the law; a small flag, a military career. A small rolling pin foretells a henpecked husband or a domineering wife. Select those objects and fortunes suitable for your group.

Soup Fortunes

Get the small letters used in alphabet soup and place them in a shallow pan of water. Let the players fish out a letter with a bent pin. The letter might indicate the initial of the person's future mate. Or you might have the letter stand for occupations. *A,* aviator; *B,* beggar; *C,* carpenter; *D,* dressmaker; *E,* elephant trainer; *F,* flier; and others.

Apple-Peeling Fortune

The old apple-peeling fortune is always popular. Give each player an apple and a knife. When the peeling breaks, he tosses it over his left shoulder. The initial formed will be that of his lover. If the peeling does not break, it indicates the person will never marry.

A THANKSGIVING PARTY

Let us come before his presence with thanksgiving.

THANKSGIVING DAY is one of the truly great American holidays. It has come to mean a time of family gatherings and of feasting. However, we must always remember it is a day set aside to give thanks to God for the many blessings He has bestowed upon us.

Since Thanksgiving Day is traditionally a time for family dinners, these suggestions might be used either at a dinner or at a November party in which you feature the Thanksgiving theme.

INVITATIONS

We do have an abundance of good things in our land, so why not make our invitations in the form of a cornucopia—The Horn of Plenty. Cut it from tan paper and draw in lines with brown crayon. Fill the horn with pictures of bright-colored foods which may be found in advertisements. Make an ear of corn and slip it into a slit in the Horn of Plenty. On this ear of corn write, "Lend an ear. We want you to come to our Thanksgiving party (or dinner) and help us give thanks for our blessings."

DECORATIONS AND FAVORS

Even in our decorations and favors we have an abundance of suggestions.

Autumn leaves make such pretty bouquets for Thanksgiving. Gather the leaves before they get too dry, place them under a sheet of waxed paper and run a warm iron over the paper. This gives the leaves a brighter gloss.

Gourds that have been dried, polished, shellacked, or enameled, ears of red corn, polished apples, nuts wrapped in tin foil, pine cones, and pumpkins may be gathered for Thanksgiving decorating.

Most tables are so heavily laden with food, that there is little room for an elaborate centerpiece. A wooden bowl filled with polished fruit and brightened with autumn leaves and bittersweet will look attractive. A small Horn of Plenty has become a tradition at our home. Sometimes this Horn conceals small favors for our younger guests. An unusual Horn of Plenty may be made from a squash gourd which has been hollowed out and dried. A pumpkin cleaned out and lined with waxed paper may be used to hold fruit or autumn leaves and bittersweet. A bouquet of mums or chrysanthemums is appropriate for a November centerpiece too.

The children might enjoy making a centerpiece for the dining table, for the buffet, or for an extra display. This could be a replica of our first Thanksgiving. Tiny log cabins may be built of small sticks glued together. Clothespin dolls may be dressed as Pilgrims and Indians. A wigwam may be fashioned by tying a bunch of dry corn husks together in a tepee shape. Make the forest by sticking sprigs of evergreen in molding clay. Tiny animals from the children's toy box could be placed in the forest. If you have a lighted church in your Christmas decorations, place this at the edge of the Pilgrim village. If not, the children can make a church similar to the log cabins. A steeple will distinguish the church from the homes.

Turkey for Favors or Decorations

Use turkeys as decorations, favors, or place cards. Here are a few simple ways to make these. The children can do this handwork.

1. Pine Cone Turkeys

A small pine cone forms the body. Use real feathers for the tail. The head and neck are made of brown paper while a bit of red candle wax may form the comb and waddle. Legs are made of pipe cleaners and the feet may be wax.

2. Shell Turkeys

If you have access to sea shells, use a shell for the turkey's body. Fill the back of the shell with cotton and glue and then press a length of pipe cleaner into this. Part of the cleaner extends to form the neck and two pieces extend for the legs. Glue a fan-shaped shell for the tail. Two small shells form the feet and these are glued to a shell base. Cotton filled with glue will hold the shells more securely than just glue alone. A pointed shell forms the head. A touch of ink and red nail polish will add features. These are not difficult but should be held firmly a few minutes until the quick-drying glue sets.

3. Cork Turkeys

A small cork forms the turkey's body. Make a slit in the cork and add brown construction paper head and tail. Pipe cleaners form the legs.

4. Other Turkeys

A prune or an oval-shaped chocolate may form the turkey's body while tail, neck, and head will be fashioned from brown paper. A few real feathers will add brightness. The ruffly paper that holds chocolates or bonbons make ideal turkey fantails.

A bright modern whimsical turkey may have a bright marshmallow for a body. Toothpicks may be used for legs, and when stuck in a bright gumdrop base, they not only hold the turkey but will carry out a color scheme.

5. Doll Favors

Thanksgiving dolls make dainty favors too. String cranberries on toothpicks for arms and legs, and stick these into the gumdrop body. Add a small gumdrop for the head. Cloves will make the nose and eyes while a red dot forms the mouth.

6. Wishbone Dolls

Save the wishbones and have them very dry and clean.

Wrap white cloth around the end to form a doll's head. Extend a pipe cleaner below this to form shoulders and arms. Cut a white circular piece of cloth and gather it from the center slit to form a dress. Make little black capes. Use pencil to draw in the features. Bits of yarn may form the hair and tiny black scarfs or hats may be fashioned.

A Thanksgiving Reminder

At every plate place a tiny cellophane bag containing five grains of corn. If real corn is used add one or two red grains. Candy corn will appeal to the children. Tie each sack with an orange and brown bow to which attach this note: "For these we give thanks." By adding a name, these will very well serve as place cards too.

When the guests are seated tell them briefly again the legend of the Pilgrims whose food supply was so depleted that only five grains were allowed each person. For these five meager grains, the Pilgrims gave thanks knowing that God could give the increase.

Ask each guest to enumerate his five greatest blessings of the year. When each person begins telling his blessings, there will be a real spirit of thanksgiving and it will be with truly grateful hearts that everyone gives thanks and sings, "Praise God from whom all blessings flow."

REFRESHMENTS

If your Thanksgiving entertainment is a family dinner, then of course you will have the traditional turkey and other dishes that your family desires.

However, if you are entertaining at a party, you may wish to serve some special Thanksgiving refreshments.

Pumpkin pie seems as truly traditional as the turkey. Serve the pie with whipped cream but top it with a tiny pumpkin made of soft cheese. Use a toothpick to make the lines and add a clove stem.

For a pretty salad, place half a pear, rounded side up, on lettuce. Cover the entire pear with halves of Tokay grapes cut lengthwise. This will look like a cluster of grapes. (To keep grapes in place, you may use cream cheese.) Add a green leaf and stem.

Doughnuts and coffee or hot chocolate may be fancied up a bit. Cover the doughnut with dark chocolate frosting and put a scoop of orange sherbet in the center. Top hot chocolate with an orange-colored marshmallow.

Bring out your turkey and pumpkin-shaped cooky cutters for cookies or sandwiches.

Serve ice cream with a turkey frozen in the center.

GAMES

Hunt the Turkey

Cut out many letters used in spelling "Turkey" and hide these about the room. At a given signal, players begin to hunt the turkeys. When time is called, the players see who can spell "turkey" the largest number of times using each letter just once.

Thanksgiving Scramble

Prepare many small slips of paper containing letters of the alphabet. Make enough so that each player will have at least fifty. See who can make the most words from his letters—each word having at least three letters. Score one point for each word and count ten points for the word *thanks*.

Let's Talk Turkey

Each question may be answered with a part of a turkey.

1. Which part would sister carry in her purse? _____ (Comb)
2. Which part does father dread at the end of the month? _____ (Bills)
3. What part would a musician use? _____ (Drumstick)
4. How does brother sometimes eat? _____ (Gobbles)
5. What part does a farmer harvest? _____ (Crop)

88

6. Which part would a carpenter use? _____ (Feet)
7. What part would you study in language? _____
   (Claws [clause])
8. What part is found on a plane? _____ (Wings)
9. What part is a story? _____ (Tail [tale])
10. What part do you do at the Thanksgiving table? _____
    (Stuffing)

First Thanksgiving

Select several objects or pictures of objects which should remind a person of the first Thanksgiving. You might include a Bible, corn, turkey or turkey feather, Indian, Pilgrim, boat, trees, gun, deer, pumpkin, log cabin, pie, and so on. Let the players study the list for awhile and then see who can remember the most.

What's Cooking?

Do you know what Mother is fixing for Thanksgiving dinner? Unscramble the foods and find out what's cooking.

1. Sings red   _____   (Dressing)
2. Pup nik m   _____   (Pumpkin)
3. Fit ur   _____   (Fruit)
4. Yet ruk   _____   (Turkey)
5. R Ben Rise Car   _____   (Cranberries)
6. Ecka   _____   (Cake)
7. Stoop eat   _____   (Potatoes)
8. Reel cy   _____   (Celery)
9. Me time cane   _____   (Mince meat)
10. Fecfeo   _____   (Coffee)

Let Us Be Thankful

The first person tells one thing for which he is thankful. The next person repeats and adds another. The third person repeats the first two and adds the thing for which he is thankful. See how long this can continue.

A CHRISTMAS PARTY

When they saw the star, they rejoiced!

A Christmas party is one of the easiest parties to plan and prepare. The holiday season is one of the most joyous times of the year, and everyone seems to be always in a festive mood and ready for a bit of added gaiety.

There is very little extra work necessary in decorating because the family's own tree, the gay wreaths, tinkling bells, poinsettias, and holly are sufficient for any type of party.

But with all of the fun and celebrating during this time of the year, we want to remember the true meaning of the day and take time to honor the Christ-child whose birthday we recall.

Invitations

Easy-to-do invitations may be written on Christmas stationery which is quite inexpensive and very decorative. However, children would enjoy helping with the party plans and perhaps would make the invitations. Let them cut stockings from bright red construction paper and tuck the invitation "inside." Very attractive are stockings cut from red felt and decorated with tiny sequins. These will hold the invitation, but by stitching a tiny safety pin on the back, they could be worn as a little lapel ornament during the holidays. You might include these lines:

This little stocking
  So bright and so gay;
Tells of a party
  On next Saturday.
So plan to attend;
  We'll play and we'll sing;

90

And honor the birthday
Of the heavenly King.

DECORATIONS AND REFRESHMENTS

Regular Christmas decorations will help create a party atmosphere.

If you do not have a traditional Christmas tablecloth, you might like to make one. This could be used for many years. Use a bright red piece of Indian Head material or you may dye a sheet. Let the children help decorate it as you may choose. We like to add a border of Christmas trees and snowflakes cut out of felt. The felt trees are decorated with beads, sequins, and bits of tinsel. These are merely tacked on and stored for another year. (The bright cloth may be used for other holidays featuring red in the color scheme.)

If you prefer a plain white cloth, cut poinsettia leaves from heavy red paper or oilcloth and use them for place mats. Bright red and green napkins add much color and these are made inexpensively from old sheets dyed. In the corner of each napkin tie a tiny jingle bell with a bit of contrasting yarn or ribbon.

Edible place cards are always enjoyed by the children. To make a simple little tree, wrap a cone-shaped drinking cup with green paper or ribbon. Tie on a few candies, add the name, and you have a place card and favor combined. Large pine cones painted green and attached firmly to a heavy cardboard base make realistic-looking trees, and candy may also be tied to these. Take three candy canes, tie them together, with curved sides down, and they become a candleholder.

For a party for "oldsters" you will find a centerpiece easily created by piling evergreen branches on a mirror. Add snow and icicles and then pile high with shiny red apples, nuts wrapped in foil, grapes, oranges, and other edibles. Make matching place cards by using sprigs of evergreen, tie on a Christmas tree ornament with the guest's name printed on the ornament in red nail polish.

A Santa sleigh makes an attractive centerpiece, and the children have fun making this too. Make the sleigh from a cardboard box, cut sides from another piece of cardboard and glue them to the box. You may paint the sleigh bright red and trim it with gilt. Santa will surely hold the reins. Use tiny plastic reindeer or reindeer candles. If none of these are available, make the deer from heavy cardboard and paint them brown. Use brown cord or shoelace for the reins. Your guests will be pleasantly surprised when you open the sleigh and distribute candy or favors to each.

Usually each family has its own traditional Christmas food so it seems unnecessary to dwell upon refreshments. However, I have found one idea which seems to please all ages and gets away from the extra-rich foods. Make sandwiches shaped like bells, trees, wreaths, and other appropriate designs. Then serve candle salad. Here is how to make it. Set the red gelatin in well-oiled baby food cans. Turn these out on very finely shredded lettuce. Roll tiny bits of cheese to represent the flames.

Plain butter cookies with hot chocolate, coffee, or punch are festive if the cookies are served on a large tray decorated with sprigs of evergreen and few tiny tree ornaments.

Even if you serve a main meal, serve a cooky tray later. Take the guests into the room that has only the glowing lights from the tree. Let them munch on the cookies while the Christmas story is read. Sing some favorite carols also.

GAMES

A Christmas Quiz

Fill in the following blanks and you will have words pertaining to the Christmas story. You may make simple lists for children and more difficult ones for the adults.

1. C_____ (Christ)
2. H_____ (Herod)
3. R_____ (Redeemer)
4. I_____ (Inn)

5. S_____ (Star)
6. T_____ (Tidings)
7. M_____ (Manger)
8. A _____ (Angels)
9. S_____ (Shepherds)

Christmas from A to Z

Ask each person to go from *A* to *Z* through the alphabet and think of a Christmas word beginning with each letter of the alphabet. *X, U, Q, Z,* may be omitted. For example you might have Angels, Bethlehem, Christ, David, East, Frankincense, Gold, Herod, Inn, Jesus, King, Light, Mary, Night, One, Peace, Redeemer, Star, Taxes, Virgin, Wise Men, Z (may stand for Zion) .

Exchanging Gifts

If you are exchanging gifts, or if you have provided small gifts, you may distribute them this way. Number each gift. Then take a ball of cord and start winding a ball. From time to time include a number that will be on the present. When seated, give the first person the ball and ask him to unwind it until he finds a number. He will take the present with the corresponding number. This continues until each person has found a number and received his gift.

The Christmas Story

Young and old alike enjoy the Christmas story. For the children you must tell the story simply. If you have a crèche give each child an object to set in place at the proper time. As you tell the story, have a list of carols to be sung as the corresponding Scriptures are read.

The Lost Toy

Arrange about twelve small toys on a table and ask the children to look at them closely. One child goes out of the room and a toy is removed. The child enters and tries to name the missing toy.

If you wish to give inexpensive toys to the children, you may place them on the table and as each child guesses the missing toy correctly it becomes his. As soon as he receives his toy he sits and waits until the others guess their toy.

What's in the Stocking?

This is a guessing game. Ask each person to tell what he would like to find in his stocking. If he names an object beginning with the first letter of his name he may stay in the game. Otherwise he must drop out of the game.

It Is More Blessed to Give

It may be that your party will be such that your guests can make something to give to shut-ins, children's wards, etc. Children like to cut out bright pictures and make scrapbooks, make Christmas cards for shut-ins, or decorate napkins or tray favors to take to hospitals. Cookies could be decorated or boxes prepared to take caroling later in the evening. It is well to remember those less fortunate than we when we are having such good times ourselves. This is surely a true gift to Him who came to give Himself for us.

What's in the Stockings?

Below are some references that will tell you what Santa left in the Christmas stockings. Hand out appropriate lists and see who can find all the gifts.

For Mother:

1. Exodus 39:11 _____
2. Matthew 27:28 _____
3. Proverbs 27:9 _____
4. Ecclesiastes 12:6 _____
5. Luke 22:36 _____
6. Genesis 24:22 _____
7. Genesis 24:22 _____
8. Matthew 14:20 _____

For Father:

1. John 19:2 _____
2. Jeremiah 23:29 _____
3. Genesis 22:6 _____
4. Acts 28:13 _____
5. Matthew 5:40 _____
6. James 2:3 _____
7. Exodus 20:25 _____
8. Malachi 3:16 _____

For Sister:	For Brother (toy farm):
1. Daniel 5:16 _____	1. Matthew 13:30 _____
2. Jeremiah 15:7 _____	2. Luke 15:23 _____
3. Leviticus 24:2 _____	3. Psalm 147:10 _____
4. Exodus 32:2 _____	4. John 10:3 _____
5. III John 13 _____	5. Isaiah 11:7 _____
6. Ruth 4:7 _____	6. Daniel 7:8 _____
7. I Samuel 2:19 _____	7. Lamentations 2:4 _____
8. Acts 19:12 _____	8. Psalm 45:5 _____

ANSWERS

For Mother:	For Father:
1. Diamond	1. Robe
2. Robe	2. Hammer
3. Perfume	3. Knife
4. Bowl	4. Compass
5. Purse	5. Coat
6. Earring	6. Footstool
7. Bracelet	7. Tool
8. Basket	8. Book

For Sister:	For Brother:
1. Chain	1. Barn
2. Fan	2. Calf
3. Lamp	3. Horse
4. Earring	4. Sheep
5. Pen	5. Cow
6. Shoe	6. Horn
7. Coat	7. Bow
8. Handkerchief	8. Arrow

For Baby:	Answers (for Baby):
1. Song of Solomon 2:5 _____	(Apple)
2. Exodus 28:33 _____	(Bell)
3. Job 39:9 _____	(Crib)
4. Genesis 44:2 _____	(Cup)

5. Philippians 3:2 _____ (Dog)
6. Ezekiel 44:18 _____ (Bonnets)
7. Revelation 20:12 _____ (Book)
8. I Timothy 6:10 _____ (Money)

What Is on the Christmas Tree?

Cut a large tree from cardboard, and from magazines cut out about two dozen appropriate gifts. There may be dolls, rings, skates, coffee pots, razors—something for all members of the family. Paste all items on the tree. Let the players look at the tree several minutes. Then remove it and see who can write the complete list of gifts.

This Is What I Want for Christmas

This is really a game for children but the older folk might act it out with very funny results. The first child says, "This is what I want for Christmas," and he attempts to act out his desire so the others may guess it. He may crawl on all "fours" and whinny if he wishes a pony. A little girl may walk stiff-kneed to represent a walking doll. This will be most humorous if the grown-ups play too.

AN ANNOUNCEMENT PARTY

A thing was secretly brought to me.

AN ANNOUNCEMENT PARTY is a most exciting event and one that should be planned lavishly because the person honored will cherish these memories throughout her entire life.

There are various clever ways of making your announcement. Here are some suggestions.

You probably will be entertaining at a tea, luncheon, or dinner, so you may use place cards as a means of making the all-important announcement.

1. "Daisies will tell" may be the theme for your announcement. Place tiny daisy corsages at each place. If you use real flowers, tuck an artificial flower in the center and have the secret hidden in this flower.

2. "My story in a nutshell." Open English walnuts carefully and gild the shells. Tuck your announcement inside then glue the shells carefully together. Decorate the shells with sequins and tie with a bow.

3. "A little bird told me." Make bluebirds or other type of birds to fit your color scheme. Find a few fluffy feathers for his tail. Cut wings of paper and glue edge to body. Conceal your announcement under his wing.

4. "Ring out the new." Secure tiny gold bells from your local variety store. Tie gay bows on each bell and attach the guest's name. When he picks up his bell to ring it, a tiny note will fall out revealing the happy news.

5. "Keep this under your hat." A gold paper lace doily will form the brim of the hat while a tiny round box or nut cup will form the crown. Add ribbon bands, streamers, tiny

flowers or other trimming. Your printed announcement will be concealed in the crown of the hat. If you wish a more old-fashioned theme, make miniature sunbonnets to conceal the secret.

6. "The wedding ring" theme is most appropriate. Cut two bands from gold paper and fit "her" band of gold inside "his" ring. Slip your announcement between the two bands.

7. "Something for a rainy day." Tiny umbrellas are inexpensive to buy. Or you may fashion them from crepe paper using drinking straws or plastic toothpicks for the handles. When the umbrellas are opened, the news will be revealed.

8. "Heartening news." Hearts are symbolic of love and a heart theme is easy to carry out in your decorations. Fashion two hearts of red or pastel-colored paper and hold them together with a gold arrow. When the arrow is removed the hearts will fall apart revealing the secret.

9. "Good news" features a tiny mailbox made from a tiny cardboard box. When the box is opened, a miniature letter falls out and the secret is told.

10. "It's in the bag." At each place is an attractive bag holding candies. Also your announcement is "in the bag."

DECORATIONS

Your decorations will be in keeping with the particular theme you choose for your announcement. However, "hearts" are appropriate with all themes that have to do with love. Pretty streamers with hearts attached will add a festive touch to your home. Tiny strings of hearts should adorn the doorways and windows.

Use a white linen or lace tablecloth. Heart place mats may be cut from red construction paper and scalloped with the edges of paper lace doilies.

A "heart tree" centerpiece is easy to make. Paint a limb white or spray it with aluminum paint. Tie tiny red hearts to the limb.

You may also cut a heart from styrofoam, add a ruffly edge,

decorate with sequins, and tie a tiny corsage in the center. Use heart styrofoam candle holders.

Another effective centerpiece is made by fashioning two hearts of heavy wire and overlapping them to form the common "entwining hearts." Wrap the wire with gold paper or pastel-colored ribbon. Stand the hearts upright and anchor them securely in a heavy flower holder or a block of wood. Entwine vines and dainty flowers around the hearts and the base that holds them.

A large heart may make a most effective decoration if displayed in a doorway or other prominent place. Fashion a large heart from a wire hoop or from heavy wire. Take strings of Christmas lights and wind around the heart. No bright lights should detract from *this* lighted heart.

REFRESHMENTS

Quite often announcement parties are given at regular dinners and in this case you would plan such a menu to suit yourself. However, your party may be a tea or informal luncheon. In that case, you would find heart-shaped sandwiches and cookies easy to decorate. With a doughnut cutter you could also make "wedding ring" sandwiches and cookies. Cream cheese tinted a deeper yellow would make the sandwich resemble the golden wedding band. Cookies should have yellow frosting. Salads could be made in heart-shaped molds.

Use a fancy cake at either type of party. A wedding ring cake could be baked in a ring mold. Frost in delicate golden shades and decorate with fancy swirls and delicately tinted flowers. Place on a large plate with the scalloped edges of paper lace doilies making a border. Place a small container in the center of the cake and add a few flowers and fernery. This could also serve as your centerpiece.

The "entwined heart" cake would make an ideal centerpiece too. Bake two heart-shaped cakes, then cut a curved section from one cake so the other heart cake would fit into the section forming the entwined hearts. Decorate the cakes and write her name on one and his on the other. Place a golden arrow through the cakes.

Found at a Wedding

These got all mixed up at the wedding. You unscramble them.

1.	Grin _____	(Ring)
2.	Gr Moo _____	(Groom)
3.	Al Rat _____	(Altar)
4.	Wolf ers _____	(Flowers)
5.	Bid er _____	(Bride)
6.	K Ace _____	(Cake)
7.	Ded Wing _____	(Wedding)
8.	Pet Rice on _____	(Reception)
9.	I C Sum _____	(Music)
10.	Sel Nice _____	(License)
11.	Bi Sired Mad _____	(Bridesmaid)
12.	L Dances _____	(Candles)

A Broken Heart

Cut hearts into six identical pieces. Mix up the pieces, distribute them, and see who can trade and mend the broken heart first.

Entwined Hearts

Draw entwined hearts on heavy construction paper and then cut them in two pieces so that only *two* will fit properly. Hide these about the room and see who can find the matching hearts first.

Biblical Announcements

Often announcements were made by angels. Below are some announcements. Can you tell to whom they were made?

1. "Thou shalt bear a son and call his name Ishmael." _____ (Hagar)
2. "Bring them out of this place for we will destroy this place." _____ (Lot)
3. "Thy prayers and thine alms are come up for a memorial before God." _____ (Cornelius)
4. "Cast thy garment about thee and follow me." _____ (Peter)
5. "The Lord is with thee, thou mighty man of valor." _____ (Gideon)
6. "Why asketh thou thus after my name seeing it is secret?" _____ (Manoah)
7. "Take the young child and his mother and flee into Egypt." _____ (Joseph)
8. "Come see the place where the Lord lay." _____ (Mary Magdalene)

The Bride's First Biscuits

Do not reveal the name of this game. This of course is just for fun! Each player numbers from one to six on her paper. On the first four lines instruct each person to write down any amount of any four ingredients. On line five, write down a container. On line six, give a descriptive word of how a person might feel. Now reveal the game. The first four items the person reads will be the ingredients the bride put in her first biscuits. The fifth line will be the container she baked them in. (Could be anything from a water bucket to a coal skuttle.) The sixth line will describe how the groom felt after partaking of the biscuits.

And They Two Shall Be One

Match the husband's name in column 1 with the wife's name in column 2.

Answers:

1. Adam	a. Hannah _____	(1—f)
2. Joseph	b. Rebekah _____	(2—g)
3. Isaac	c. Sarah _____	(3—b)
4. Jacob	d. Ruth _____	(4—h)
5. Ahasuerus	e. Drusilla _____	(5—k)
6. Ananias	f. Eve _____	(6—j)
7. Felix	g. Mary _____	(7—e)
8. Elkanah	h. Rachel _____	(8—a)
9. Zacharias	i. Naomi _____	(9—l)
10. Boaz	j. Sapphira _____	(10—d)
11. Abraham	k. Esther _____	(11—c)
12. Elimelech	l. Elisabeth _____	(12—i)

A BRIDAL SHOWER—UMBRELLA THEME

She looketh well to the ways of her household.

THERE IS SOMETHING VERY EXTRA SPECIAL about a bridal shower and the memories of it will repay all the time and effort you put into your planning this important party.

When one thinks of showers she thinks of umbrellas so here is a plan for an *umbrella shower* for the bride.

INVITATIONS

The invitations will be in the shape of tiny parasols cut from pastel-colored paper. Sketch the details with black ink. Add handles of black paper. Make the umbrella part double so the umbrella may be opened to reveal the following invitation:

> This wee umbrella comes to say,
> "There's going to be a shower
> On Mary Smith who met her fate";
> Please don't forget the hour.

DECORATIONS

You will surely want to use umbrellas in your decorations. So many real umbrellas today are pretty enough to fit in with any color scheme you may select; the toy counter will have colorful paper Japanese umbrellas. Hang umbrellas in doorways, from the center of the room, or in archways. Tiny streamers may be run from one parasol to another or tiny strings of paper flowers may cascade from each rib of the umbrella.

The bridal shower is surely the time to bring out your choice linens, china, and silverware. For a dainty centerpiece use a low glass bowl that resembles an opened umbrella turned upside down. Make a cane-shaped handle from heavy wire, cover it with crepe paper, and place it in the frog (flower holder) amid your flowers. Stand a miniature bride and groom near the umbrella.

Put a row of greenery down the center of the table and add tiny flowers. At each place, put a tiny umbrella. These usually can be purchased, but if not available you can make them quickly. Cut a circular piece of paper, then cut out a small V-shaped piece out of the circular piece. When the cut edges are glued together this takes on the shape of an umbrella. Colored straws or colored plastic toothpicks form the handles. These little umbrellas may also be attached to nut cups. Use round napkins too.

All of the gaily wrapped gifts are placed upon a table covered with a solid-colored cloth. Place an umbrella in the center of the table so the gifts lie about it. You can make an attractive umbrella by covering an old parasol with crepe paper. Around the edge add lace scallops which are merely round paper lace doilies cut in half. Wrap the handle of the umbrella and add a perky bow. To the top of the umbrella add a tiny bouquet of flowers.

REFRESHMENTS

Your refreshments must be very dainty for this party. Pastel-colored gelatin salads and sandwiches are appropriate. Make round open-faced sandwiches and use a light filling. Tint whipped cream a darker shade, put it in a cake decorator to make the ribbons on the umbrella sandwich.

To make umbrella cookies draw the outline of an umbrella on heavy paper, trace it on the rolled cooky dough and cut with a sharp knife. When cool, decorate with colored icings.

Another idea for an umbrella cooky is to bake a small round scalloped-edged cooky. Decorate it to resemble an umbrella. Then insert a plastic toothpick through the center and this parasol will rest on its side.

Ice cream or a fruit salad dessert and coffee go well with the cookies.

It Is Raining

Each player is given a large paper plate "umbrella" with a string attached so he may tie it on his head. In the center of the room is a pile of marbles, ping pong balls, or other small objects. At a given signal each player tries to pick up the objects in his spoon and put them in his "umbrella." When you call, "It's raining," the person with the most objects in his "umbrella" is winner.

A BRIDAL SHOWER—RECIPES

MOST NEW BRIDES find that planning and preparing meals is one of their major problems. A "recipe shower" could well be the answer to this problem. If the bride has been feted often, and the same guests have been included, this would be a fine informal way for you to do something just a little special.

INVITATIONS

Write your invitations to this Recipe Shower on a recipe card. Around the edges or across the top, outline pans, measuring spoons, and other kitchen utensils. Be sure to ask each guest to bring along a favorite recipe. You may avoid duplicates by suggesting a "particular" recipe. If it seems feasible in your particular group, each person might be requested to bring a recipe and the necessary kitchen utensil for preparing the recipe. For example, a cooky recipe would be attached to a cooky sheet, a salad recipe enclosed in a mold, and so on.

REFRESHMENTS

This type of shower is ideal when a club wishes to honor one of its members at a regular meeting so this might well be a co-op luncheon or meal. Perhaps each lady would like to be responsible for bringing the "made up" recipe she will give the bride.

If you do not plan a luncheon, serve recipe sandwiches. Cut slices of sandwich bread in half so they resemble cards. With tinted mayonnaise make lines and lettering to resemble a recipe card. You might tell the guests the sandwich cards include a housewife's day. On them you might print, "Wash," "Iron," "Bake," or "Mend."

Recipe for Wedded Bliss

Play this as a circle game for fun or as a paper-and-pencil game for prizes. Each recipe for wedded bliss must be an alphabetical phrase of not less than three words. Beginning with *A,* the first player might suggest, "Always Act Affectionately." The second might say, "Bake Biscuits Before Breakfast." The next might say, "Cook Cabbage Carefully."

The Bride's First Cake

When the bride started to bake her first cake she had to go shopping for some of the ingredients. Bible references will aid you in solving her shopping list.

1. "The words of his mouth were smoother than _____."
   Psalm 55:21
2. "His wife looked back . . . and she became a pillar of _____." Genesis 19:26
3. "When any will offer a meat-offering unto the Lord, his offering shall be of fine _____." Leviticus 2:1
4. "And she came to Jerusalem with a very great train, with camels that bear _____." I Kings 10:2
5. "As one gathereth _____ that are left, have I gathered all the earth." Isaiah 10:14
6. "The hills shall flow with _____." Joel 3:18

Answers

1.	Butter	4.	Spices
2.	Salt	5.	Eggs
3.	Flour	6.	Milk

If prizes are given, packets of recipe cards, inexpensive cookbooks, or even packages of cake mixes would be fitting.

As a climax to the Recipe Shower, why not present the honored guest with a recipe cabinet for all the fine recipe cards she has received.

BRIDAL SHOWER—A CUPBOARD SHOWER

A CUPBOARD SHOWER is most practical for the newly married couple who will be moving into their own home immediately following the wedding ceremony. As the name implies, each gift is in the form of food.

You may find it less confusing if you do a little planning so there is a larger variety of foods. Be sure that the cupboard is stocked with those items only remembered by the new cook when she is ready to use them. This list might include spices, cornstarch, soda, and so forth.

The spices might be presented in a spice rack; the sugar, flour, and other staples in a canister set, or in various other ways if desired.

INVITATIONS

Invitations to this shower will be in the form of a cupboard. Fold a piece of heavy white paper in half. Sketch drawers and doors to represent a cupboard. Cut out the two top doors so they will open revealing shelves on which will be written the invitation.

GAMES

What Am I?

As each guest arrives pin the name of a common kitchen object on her back. She tries to identify the object by asking questions of the other guests. Only "yes" and "no" answers may be given.

Foods That Go Together

See who can write, in a given time, the longest list of foods that go together such as salt and pepper, bacon and eggs, corned beef and cabbage, ice cream and cake, bread and butter.

The Bride's Cupboard

The bride found these things in her cupboard. What are they:

1. B dear _____ (Bread)
2. A Rugs _____ (Sugar)
3. L four _____ (Flour)
4. C Hoot Lace _____ (Chocolate)
5. O Sad _____ (Soda)
6. Ge Ring _____ (Ginger)
7. Som Sales _____ (Molasses)
8. Sat Cup _____ (Catsup)
9. Ret Tub _____ (Butter)
10. Pat Too _____ (Potato)
11. Race M _____ (Cream)
12. Shall Mar Mow _____ (Marshmallow)

BRIDAL SHOWER—RING THEME

THIS BRIDAL SHOWER theme will feature the "little band of gold."

INVITATIONS

For your invitations, cut a ring from heavy paper and gild the front of it. Write the invitation on the back. This little rhyme might be used.

> This little band of gold you see
>   Brings word to you today.
> We'll have a show'r for Mary Jones
>   Before her wedding day.

DECORATIONS AND REFRESHMENTS

Your home may be decorated with little hoops covered with gold paper. Hang tiny pastel blossoms from these rings. Hang one larger ring in a conspicuous place and from it hang satin ribbons to hold small gifts. These might be measuring spoons, cooky cutters, etc. To present the larger gifts, decorate a box to resemble a ring box and place the gifts in it. Or hide the gifts, then tie strings to the gifts and attach a ring to the other end. Give the ring to the bride-to-be and have her follow the string to each gift.

For a centerpiece arrange a bouquet in a very low container. From the center of the bouquet and slightly higher than the flowers have two entwining bands of gold—His and Hers. These may be formed by cutting two heavy rings of cardboard for each ring. Before gluing the two bands together place a circle of fine wire inside the bands and let the wire extend at the bottom to form "stems." Cover the bands with gold paper and add tiny sparkles to Her ring. Wrap the wire stems in tape and place them in the center of the bouquet. The stems are concealed showing only the wedding rings above the floral arrangement.

To carry out the "ring" theme in refreshments, serve doughnuts, sandwiches cut with doughnut cutter, ring mold salads, and wedding ring cookies.

GAMES

Kitchen Quiz

Give contestants some old magazines and scissors. They are to find pictures alphabetically of items commonly found in the kitchen. Pictures might include: *A*—apple, *B*—bread, *C*—canisters, *D*—dishes, and on through the alphabet.

Calling All Husbands

If you want a silly game, have the old-fashioned husband-calling contest. Be sure there are no cops walking the beat!

Describing the Bride and Groom

Each player is to write a description of both the bride and groom using the letters in their first name. For example, if the bride is Mary, a player might say she is Meek, Alluring, Rebellious, and Young. If the groom's name is John, he will be Jolly, Obedient, Henpecked, Neat.

Match the wives and husbands.

				Answers:
1.	Naomi	a.	Ahaz _____	(1—j)
2.	Zipporah	b.	Agrippa _____	(2—d)
3.	Ruth	c.	Herod _____	(3—i)
4.	Bernice	d.	Moses _____	(4—b)
5.	Priscilla	e.	Ahasuerus _____	(5—h)
6.	Jezebel	f.	Jacob _____	(6—a)
7.	Esther	g.	Joseph _____	(7—e)
8.	Herodias	h.	Aquila _____	(8—c)
9.	Leah	i.	Boaz _____	(9—f)
10.	Asenath	j.	Elimelech _____	(10—g)

Mock Weddings

A mock wedding is always lots of fun if you choose those guests who will carry on in a humorous way.

Picture This Love Story

Here are eight poems. Give the players paper and pencil and tell them to illustrate each poem. Or you may distribute magazines and let them find illustrations. Give a prize to the one who has the most humorous pictured story.

1. This is the story of bride and of groom;
   Here are their pictures that hang in the room.

2. When they were courting they'd ride around town—
   This is the vehicle—sight most renown.

3. He finally proposed one moonlighted night;
   Here is the pose—romantic sight?

4. They went to the preacher to say, "I do."
   A handsome young pair, I think. Don't you?

5. This is the home where they both settled down,
   In this little section of our fine town.

6. Now they have children to brighten their day,
   Here is their picture—all at their play.

7. He promised her diamonds, a maid or two,
   Do you think she did get them? Oh, show us, do!

8. Years have rolled by like the fast moving brook;
   Now see them again—here's a final wee look.

BABY SHOWER—ROCK-A-BYE BABY

Unto us a Child is born.

A BABY SHOWER provides the right occasion to go extremely fussy or "cute" in your planning. There are a variety of themes one might follow in planning such an important party. I shall give you a few suggestions and you may alter them to suit your particular group.

A Rock-A-Bye Baby Shower

Any mother will surely sing the old favorite "Rock-a-Bye, Baby" lullaby so why not use this theme in your planning?

INVITATIONS

Our invitations will be in the form of a little old-fashioned cradle. Make these in pink or blue, then paste an edging of lace and add tiny pink and blue bows. Make the cradle double so you can include this invitation on the inside:

> Rock-a-bye, baby,
> In the tree top,
> When the wind blows
> The cradle will rock.
> When the bow bends
> The cradle will fall,
> Down came the Baby,
> Cradle, and all.

DECORATIONS AND REFRESHMENTS

Let the Rock-A-Bye tree be the center of your decorating scheme. If your shower is in warm weather, you may use a flowering branch for the tree. Otherwise spray a limb white and attach pink and blue blossoms or bows. From the branch, hang a tiny doll cradle with a baby doll in a blanket. This may be presented to the honored guest later.

Place the gifts under the tree. If the new baby is a first child, it might be well if several guests combined their money and bought a bassinet to put under the tree.

Serve your favorite refreshments but carry out the "pink and blue" color scheme. Cake and coffee with mints make ample refreshments. To make an attractive serving, bake loaf angel food cakes and cut the pieces into irregular shapes then cover half of them with pale blue frosting and the other pieces in pink. Decorate the blue with pink buds and green leaves and the pink pieces in blue buds with green leaves. Place all of these on a large silver tray and serve them. In warm weather, you may prefer pink lemonade instead of coffee. Serve pink and white mints.

To carry out the "Rock-A-Bye-Baby" theme in your serving, place a tiny plastic tree or a tiny branch in pink and blue gumdrops. On each tree, tie a tiny rubber doll wrapped in pink or blue blanket.

GAMES
"Down Came the Baby, Cradle, and All."

Each person is given 10 tiny cradles and at a given signal searches the room to find tiny baby pictures to fit into each cradle. The first person to find a missing baby for each cradle is winner.

What Is in the Cradle?

Use a doll cradle or bassinet and fill it with numerous items commonly used in caring for a baby, such as safety pins, bottle, soap, swabs, oil, powder, and so on. Empty the cradle in front of the guests and allow them to study the contents for a few minutes. Remove the items and see who can write the most accurate list.

Moses in the Cradle

Give each player paper and pencil and see who can answer the most questions correctly concerning Moses.

1. Moses' mother was named _____. (Jochebed)
2. Moses was placed in an ark made of _____. (Bulrushes)
3. It was daubed with _____ and _____. (Slime and pitch)
4. _____ sought to kill all sons. (Pharaoh)
5. Moses was found by _____. (Pharaoh's daughter)
6. Moses' sister was named _____. (Miriam)
7. The name Moses means _____. (Drawn out of the water or saved from the water)
8. Aaron was Moses' _____. (Brother)
9. Amran was Moses' _____. (Father)
10. When Moses lived in the palace of Pharaoh, his nurse was _____. (Moses' mother)

(You may find other games at the end of this chapter on Baby Showers.)

BABY SHOWER—A-NEW-HEIR-TO-THE-THRONE THEME

Iᶠ ʏᴏᴜ ᴀʀᴇ ᴛɪʀᴇᴅ of the proverbially "pink and blue" type of shower, you may enjoy this type of shower for the new heir.

Iɴᴠɪᴛᴀᴛɪᴏɴs

If there is to be a new ruler, there must be a new crown, so let us make a crown from a folded sheet of heavy gold paper. The jewels may be pink and blue sequins glued in fancy designs or you may use tiny pink and blue gummed seals such as is used for decorating Easter eggs. These will be found at your local stationery counter or the children may have a package left over from Easter.

Your invitation might read as follows:

> Today our Mary is the ruler,
> A Queen of great renown,
> But soon a brand-new heir will come
> To usurp her jeweled crown.

Dᴇᴄᴏʀᴀᴛɪᴏɴs

One of the gifts might include a high chair, a stroller, or other type of chair for the baby. This could bear a sign, "Throne for the Heir." Decorate it with such useful "jewels" as rattles, teething rings, chains of safety pins, or little toys.

The "Queen's Throne" might be placed beside this little throne. This of course would be a comfortable chair for your honored guest. Decorate it lavishly with pink and blue ribbon streamers and bows. These will come in handy later for use on little sweaters and bonnets.

A centerpiece for this party could be in the form of a Royal Chest for the Royal Jewels. Paint a small box or cover it with gold paper. Search through your discarded jewelry for "glitter." Glue these "gems" on the box. Or if you wish to be more practical, paint a box in pink or blue and add nursery decals. Fill the chest with inexpensive items for the Royal Heir. Include pins, tiny bottles of baby oil, powder, or similar items. The new mother will find the little chest very handy.

REFRESHMENTS

Depend upon pink and blue food colorings to carry through the proverbial color scheme. On cookies or cakes use plenty of silver shot and colored sugars to give a "jeweled" effect to frostings.

Open-faced sandwiches may be topped with crowns made of thin slices of cheese. Half-slices of pineapple rings in salad will serve for crowns.

GAMES

For paper-and-pencil games, present each guest with a sheet of paper that has a crown in the corner. Begin each instruction with "Her Majesty requests" or "The Queen demands."

Naming the Heir

Selecting a name for the Royal Arrival is a momentous occasion. You will help the Queen by selecting a name for either a Prince or Princess. Each feminine name must begin with the mother's initials and the masculine name with the father's initials. For example, if the mother's name is Mary Smith and her husband is John Smith, you might suggest the names of Marcia Sue and John Samuel. You will be amused at the variety of names discovered.

Gifts Fit for a King

What do you think these people in the Bible might bring to the new Heir? Match the gifts and the giver.

Answers:

1.	Abel	a.	Silver cup _____	(1—d)
2.	Hannah	b.	Ointment _____	(2—i)
3.	David	c.	Gold, frankincense, myrrh _____	(3—j)
4.	Noah	d.	Sheep _____	(4—h)
5.	Benjamin	e.	Apple _____	(5—a)
6.	Eve	f.	Bracelets _____	(6—e)
7.	Wise Men	g.	Coat of many colors _____	(7—c)
8.	Mary	h.	Ark _____	(8—b)
9.	Abraham's servant	i.	Coat _____	(9—f)
10.	Joseph	j.	Harp _____	(10—g)

Greeting the New Heir

This is an idea just for fun. Wrap a gift and tell the mother-to-be she is to keep this package and guard it carefully. Then have each guest write the day and the hour when she thinks the new Heir will arrive. Sign her name. These papers are put into an envelope, sealed and made sure with the Royal Seal (which is a gold seal or stamp). Instruct the mother-to-be that after the Heir has come, she is to open this envelope. She will notify the lady who had the most accurate date. When that person goes to "pay homage" to the new Heir she will receive the mystery package which is her award.

Famous Mothers and Sons from the Bible

1. What mother and son were related to Mary, the mother of Jesus? _____ (Elisabeth and John the Baptist)
2. Who was the first mother and son? _____ (Eve and Cain)

3. What mother and son saw each other only yearly? _____ _____ (Hannah and Samuel)
4. What mother and son deceived their husband and father? _____ (Rebekah and Jacob)
5. What mother and son were favorites of Jacob? _____ (Rachel and Joseph)
6. What mother and son were known for their knowledge of the Scriptures? _____ (Eunice and Timothy)
7. What mother and son were the beginning of the great race of people chosen by God? _____ (Sarah and Isaac)
8. What mother lost her son when they came from worshiping? _____ (Mary and Jesus)
9. What mother and son were taken to Pharaoh's palace? _____ (Jochebed and Moses)
10. What mother and son were cast out? _____ (Hagar and Ishmael)

He Shall Have Music

You will need a piano to play this game. These songs should help name the new arrival. Play songs with names in them and see who can identify them first. There are such old favorites as "Jeanie with the Light Brown Hair," "Sweet Genevieve," "Rosie O'Grady," "Alice Blue Gown," "Danny Boy," and others.

Serving the New Heir

The person who serves the Heir must be very strong and not short of wind. Each person is given a balloon. Inside each balloon is a tiny piece of paper telling where the Royal Gems are hidden. The person who can blow up his balloon, burst it, and get the directions, may hurry and find the hidden prize.

Name the Nursery Rhyme

Every mother should know the familiar nursery rhymes. From magazines cut pictures suggestive of well-known nursery rhymes, number them, and see who can identify the most correctly. This is a suggestive list.

1. Kettle _____ ("Polly Put the Kettle on")
2. Black sheep _____ ("Baa, Baa, Black Sheep")
3. Flower garden _____ ("Mary, Mary, Quite Contrary")
4. An old shoe _____ ("There Was an Old Woman Who Lived in a Shoe")
5. Candlestick _____ ("Jack Be Nimble")
6. Spider _____ ("Little Miss Muffet")
7. Horn and sheep _____ ("Little Boy Blue")
8. A Pig _____ ("Tom, Tom, the Piper's Son")
9. Sheep and school _____ ("Mary Had a Little Lamb")
10. Water pail _____ ("Jack and Jill")
11. A pie _____ ("Little Jack Horner")

Making a Layette

Use a catalog and make a list of the items included in a common layette. See who can write the most accurate list using the catalog list as a standard.

SUGGESTIONS

Often older ladies do not care to participate in games. For them, visiting is more enjoyable. You may provide some blocks of pink and blue and let them embroider a design on each block. These blocks are quickly stitched together into a little coverlet for baby's bed.

WEDDING ANNIVERSARIES

*For this cause shall a man leave his father and mother
and shall be joined unto his wife.*

WEDDING ANNIVERSARIES are very special, although we
usually stress the twenty-fifth and the fiftieth. However, families and neighbors often enjoy celebrating those
"in-between" anniversaries too.

Here is some information which will be of help in planning any anniversary.

First—Paper	Ninth—Pottery	Twenty-fifth—Silver
Second—Cotton	Tenth—Tin	Thirtieth—Pearl
Third—Leather	Eleventh—Steel	Thirty-fifth—Coral
Fourth—Flowers	Twelfth—Linen	Fortieth—Ruby
Fifth—Wooden	Thirteenth—Lace	Forty-fifth—Sapphire
Sixth—Candy	Fourteenth—Ivory	Fiftieth—Golden
Seventh—Copper	Fifteenth—Crystal	Fifty-fifth—Emerald
Eighth—Bronze	Twentieth—China	Seventy-fifth—Dia-mond

Space would not permit us to plan every anniversary.
However, with suggestions for the outstanding years, you
will be able to carry out plans for any of the years you wish
to celebrate.

First

Now let us consider the First anniversary which is Paper.
When a young couple has weathered the first year and come
through with flying colors, it calls for a celebration. And
since this anniversary is the very first, it will be marked more
by gaiety than by sentiment or memories. This is an ideal
time for a group of young married couples to get together

for an informal good time. What could make for easier entertainment than paper tablecloth, dishes, napkins, and even a centerpiece of artificial flowers? This would be a fine occasion for a co-op or pot-luck meal. Even paper sack lunches would be in keeping with the "paper" theme.

Gifts for the married couple might include paper towels, napkins, stationery, subscriptions to magazines, books, or other forms of paper gifts.

Fifth

The Fifth anniversary is the Wooden one. Arrange a floral centerpiece in a wooden bowl and on either side place candles in wooden candle holders. Children's wooden blocks may be painted white and on them print in red, the letters to spell out "Happy Anniversary." Arrange these artistically across the table or around the centerpiece.

Another idea for a wooden centerpiece would be the proverbial wooden rolling pin. Cut out the center and fill with flowers. If you wish to present it to the couple later, or as a prize, keep it intact and entwine a vine and tiny flowers around the pin. Tie gay bows on the handles. For place cards or favors, purchase a child's small wooden rolling pin and print the guest's name in bright colors.

Gifts may range from inexpensive wooden plaques or salad bowls to a piece of furniture.

Tenth

The Tenth anniversary is Tin, so what could be more appropriate than tin cans? For an easy-to-do centerpiece, dress small dolls to represent a bride and groom. Use a small toy car and tie tiny tin cans on it. Of course you will print "Just Married" on the car. In smaller letters print "ten years."

If you wish to have a centerpiece that is more artistic, you may wish to make a tin tree. Secure a clean shiny half-gallon tin can. Remove the ends, then cut down the side of the can opposite the seam. Now starting at the top of the can, cut as many ¼ inch strips as possible. Bend the strips to represent branches and attach a crepe paper flower on the end of each. Add a few green leaves, too. Set this tree firmly in a shiny can filled with sand.

Small cans such as baby-food cans may serve as nut cups. If you print the guest's name in bright nail polish or with enamel, the nut cups may double as place cards. Silver paper lace doilies will help carry out the "tin" effect. You might even serve your guests on bright tin plates and use tin cups.

An appropriate gift for the married couple might be a pantry shower—tins of food.

Fifteenth

The Fifteenth anniversary is Crystal, so this tends to be more elaborate. This calls for your best linens, china, and silverware. You will use crystal vases, candleholders, and glassware to make your table take on the crystal look that is necessary for the fifteenth year.

A low glass bowl filled with roses, sweet peas, or other dainty flowers will form the centerpiece. Candles to harmonize with your color scheme will add that soft glow to make your table look even more enchanting. Tiny glass nut cups with pastel-colored mints add a sparkle. Or you may use paper nut cups covered with clear cellophane and tied with a tiny flower and bow. There are very inexpensive glass place cards which are reusable and they would look lovely. Sequins glued to the nut cups and some artificial snow sprinkled about will add a crystal effect to the table.

Provide a corsage for the honored guest and tiny corsages for the other ladies.

Twenty-Fifth

The Twenty-fifth is the Silver wedding anniversary and one which you no doubt will observe with open house. There are so many wonderful decorations and helps which you may purchase at a very nominal price to help you make this occasion very special.

Silver crepe paper streamers and silver bells will add a festive touch. Flowers in silver vases or bowls or in containers covered with silver paper add a bright touch.

An attractive table is easy to arrange. You may wish to choose a pastel color to use with the silver—probably the color you chose for your wedding. The table cover may be this shade and then add a border of silver rickrack or braid. This may be sewed in a straight border or you may add an artistic touch by making little rickrack hearts along the edge. The ladies who help with the serving might wear dainty organdy aprons in the chosen pastel shade, and these too would have matching borders of silver rickrack. Also provide them "cufflets" to match the apron. These should be about three or four inches wide, cut straight across the bottom and rounding at the top. A row of rickrack will trim these and then add the silver gummed numerals "25."

Often the family presents silver dollars to the honored couple. This could be presented on a "silver tree," which could also serve as a centerpiece. Take an ordinary branch and spray it with silver paint. Tie the silver dollars to the branches using ribbon to carry out the color scheme. From the tree, down the center of the table place silver leaves with tiny pastel-colored flowers.

For another type of centerpiece, you may feature a silver "25." Use three-tiered boxes for the base. Cover each with silver paper, ruffles, bows, or flowers to make it really attractive. Cover the entire top box with tiny flowers. Fashion a heart-shaped wreath of silver leaves and stand it upright on the top box. Suspended from the center top of the wreath is a silver "25." This may be made of cardboard and painted or covered with silver paper.

For such an anniversary, cake, ice cream, mints and nuts, punch and coffee seem to be the accepted refreshments.

Provide a book so the guests may register. At an open house there is usually no need for any entertainment since greetings and visiting take care of the time. However, you may provide soft music if you wish.

The Fiftieth anniversary is indeed the Golden year and this should be an occasion that will be long remembered. However, at the outset may I suggest that you first take into consideration the physical condition and the wishes of the honored couple. Do not plan an elaborate occasion if they would prefer a simpler family type get-together. Do not plan such an elaborate affair that the end of the day finds the couple more exhausted than happy.

All that has been suggested for the twenty-fifth anniversary might very well be duplicated in "gold" for the fiftieth anniversary.

Here again you will find gold-colored paper doilies, yellow nut cups, and special napkins inexpensive.

If you wish to add an extra touch to your table, or give little remembrances of this occasion, this is easy to do. Purchase real or artificial yellow rosebuds or baby roses and a bit of greenery. Make a dainty corsage, add a gold ribbon bow to each, and on the streamers attach a gold numeral "50" which comes in the gummed seals.

At a dinner, these corsages could have a name attached and serve as place cards.

Put the gummed numerals on the clear glasses too. For another type of place card use a folded piece of white paper, and in one corner tie a tiny golden bell.

For your centerpiece use yellow flowers in crystal containers and have yellow candles in crystal holders. Above the center of the table have streamers with a golden wedding bell caught in the center.

Provide comfortable chairs for the guests. Even the old photograph album should be brought out for this occasion. And do bring out the wedding pictures.

Wedding anniversaries are cherished by a happily married couple, so make theirs a memorable occasion whether it be the first or the fiftieth.

A FAREWELL PARTY

*The Lord watch between me and thee, when we are
absent one from another.*

A FAREWELL PARTY is a very nice gesture and one the departing person will appreciate. I am suggesting a "Blue
Party" for this. However, if the party is for a younger person who may be moving from the neighborhood reluctantly,
keep the party in a lighter mood and do not emphasize the
fact that he must leave.

INVITATIONS

Make your invitations on folded blue paper. On the front
draw a scowling little face to accompany the lines;

> You know that we feel blue;
> Since Mary's going away:

Then on the next page draw a happy face to accompany the
lines:

> But we are giving a party
> To brighten up our day.

SUGGESTIONS

Use a white table cover with bouquets of blue flowers. If
these are not available, use a blue cover and have a small
chest, trunk, or miniature suitcase for a centerpiece. This
might contain a small gift for the friend. Nut cups could
be in blue, and the place cards could be white with little
blue forget-me-nots sketched across one corner.

If you have blue dishes, use them. Or perhaps you have
some blue bowls which could be used in serving.

Blue food-coloring will help you carry out your color

scheme. Cakes cut into oblong pieces can be decorated like a trunk or suitcase.

When presenting a farewell gift, you may be able to carry through your blue color scheme. There might be blue linens, handkerchiefs, jewelry, tie clasps with blue sets, shirts or blouses, or any number of items that could carry out the "blue" idea.

A "memory gift" is always appreciated. Children enjoy these popular "autograph hounds." A lady might enjoy a set of quilt blocks with her friends' names on the blocks. This could be made into a friendship quilt. Even a set of dish-towels with names embroidered in the corner would be nice. A boy could have an autographed baseball or football. An address book with the names and addresses of the friends would surely be a useful gift.

GAMES

Let's Get Ready to Move

Pack suitcases with clothing and give one suitcase to each team. A player must put on all the apparel, run to a designated spot, remove the clothes, and put them back in the suitcase; then he runs back to the line and gives the suitcase to the next player who does likewise. The first team through is the winner. Make this a really hilarious game by putting women's clothing in the men's suitcase and vice versa. Teenaged boys in baby bonnets won't remain dignified very long.

What Will They Take When They Move?

This may be a circle game. The first player names an object and an adjective beginning with *A* that Mary will take when she moves. It might be her Antique Armchair; for *B*, her Beloved Broom; for *C*, her Children's Cat; for *D*, Dirty Dishes, and so on through the alphabet. Skip *X*, *Z*.

Here Is What Mary Will Take

In a small cloth bag, place about two dozen objects that Mary will take when she moves. Make the objects suitable to the individual. Allow the players so many minutes to feel what is in the sack. The one who can list the contents most correctly is winner.

Where Did They Go?

Many people of the Bible moved. Can you match these correctly?

Answers:

1. Jacob	a. Bethlehem _____	(1—g)
2. Mary and Joseph	b. Damascus _____	(2—a)
3. Naomi	c. Egypt _____	(3—j)
4. Paul	d. Jerusalem _____	(4—b)
5. Wise Men	e. Land of Canaan _____	(5—d)
6. Israelites	f. Patmos _____	(6—e)
7. John	g. Haran _____	(7—f)
8. Jonah	h. Babylon _____	(8—i)
9. Joseph	i. Nineveh _____	(9—c)
10. Daniel	j. Moab _____	(10—h)

Write a Letter

During the evening give each person paper and pencil and tell him to write a letter to the honored guest. Seal the letters in a large envelope and tell the person she is not to open the letters until she has had her *first* meal in her new home.

Farewell

Before farewells are said, have each person tell some incident concerning the departing person that they will always remember. It may be some kind deed done or some humorous incident.

BIRTHDAY PARTY—A MYSTERY TREE

*Thou shalt have joy and gladness and many shall
rejoice at his birth.*

NOTHING IS MORE ENJOYABLE than a birthday party, and
nothing more exciting than a mystery. So when we
combine the two, we are sure of a successful party. Such a
party may be simple enough to please a small child or mysterious enough to intrigue older people.

INVITATIONS

For your invitations make a tree with brown trunk and a
solid green top. With dark crayon make the limbs and
leafy designs. Since this mystery tree is also a birthday tree,
we shall cut slits in the branches for candles. The front of
the candles will be colored but backs of them will contain
our party information.

This tree may vary according to the season, if you wish.
If the birthday comes at Easter time, you might substitute
decorated eggs for candles. For February birthdays, you
might attach hearts; for October, jack-o'-lanterns; and so on.

DECORATIONS

A Mystery Tree is a *must* at this party. If you plan an outdoor party then you may use a real tree for your mystery
tree. Make it special by tying a bright red ribbon around
it and a big bow. You might tie mysterious packages to its
limbs. Or you may place a spade beside it. Tie a bright bow
on the spade handle with this message:

I'm a great big Mystery Tree
Hiding a prize for you.

129

> Dig with this rusty, trusty spade,
> But hurry, hurry, do!

You may bury a box decorated like a pirate's chest containing balloons or favors for the guests. Or you may bury the birthday presents under the Mystery Tree.

If the party is indoors, you will have to construct a Mystery Tree. Secure a branch and anchor it firmly in a container. You may spray a bare branch, wrap it with crepe paper, or decorate it any way that is appropriate for your type of party. Have birthday gifts placed under the tree and hang special favors on the branches.

Refreshments

You may easily combine the mystery theme with your customary birthday refreshments. Bake the birthday cake in the tree pans you use at Christmas time. Decorate with pale green frosting, put birthday candles on the branches, and spell out "Happy Birthday" in white icing.

Small children like to have a candle to blow out too. Make them tree cookies. You can push a candle into the icing on these.

Cut sandwiches with your tree cooky cutter. Cover with sandwich spreads that may be tinted pale green and decorate with bits of pimento or slices of stuffed olives.

A plastic tree might be used as a centerpiece. Bright candies or flowers should adorn the branches. Place cards could be made by sticking a tiny branch into a gumdrop. Tie the name to the branch.

Games

The Leaves Have Fallen

Give each person a tree to color. This tree will have ten leaves on it. Each leaf *must* be colored. When the coloring is finished, tell the players their scores will depend upon the color of their leaves. Every green leaf will count one point, red leaves two points, yellow leaves three points, and a brown leaf five points. None of the other colors will count.

What Tree?

What tree would you find—

1. On a calendar? _____ (Date)
2. On an animal? _____ (Fir)
3. At the ocean? _____ (Beech)
4. On your hand? _____ (Palm)
5. In a bottle? _____ (Cork)
6. In front of a mirror? _____ (Spruce)
7. In oil? _____ (Olive)
8. In a stove? _____ (Ash)
9. In a canoe? _____ (Birch)
10. In a duet? _____ (Pear)

Put the Leaf Back on the Tree

Place a limb with several small branches in a weighted can and place it in the center of the floor. Tie real leaves or paper ones to fruit-jar rings and have players toss the "leaves" at the limb. Each "leaf" that hangs on a limb counts ten points.

For another version of this toss game, draw a large tree on wrapping paper and mark one branch 5, one 10, one 20, and the top one 50. Give each player five "leaves" cut from thin scraps of wood. Toss the "leaves" at the tree and total the scores.

Standing on the Mystery

Each player is given a large paper leaf which has come off the Mystery Tree and will bring him good luck so long as he stands upon it. But the Old Witch has no good luck leaf. When music is played, everyone must march about. When the music stops the Old Witch tries to find a leaf to stand upon. The person who has no leaf becomes the Old Witch. Or you may have the one without a leaf drop out of the game taking a leaf with him. This continues until only one lucky person is left to be winner.

Naming Trees

Give out paper and pencil and see who can name the most trees in a limited time. For younger children, you might ask them to name the kinds of trees they know.

Games for Young Children

Children always enjoy familiar games, so they might play "Here We Go Round the Mulberry Bush," substituting the words, "Here We Go Round the Mystery Tree."

Play "Button, Button," substituting "Who has the leaf?"

When playing drop the handkerchief, drop a leaf cut from a piece of bright-colored cloth. When you are put in the center, you are "Climbing the Mystery Tree."

Receiving Gifts

When it is time to unwrap the birthday gifts, ask everyone to sit around the Mystery Tree and sing "Happy Birthday." Everyone will enjoy the Mystery Tree because it will not only bear birthday gifts but small favors for all the guests.

If you are giving prizes for games, have them tied in interesting packages to the limbs and let the winners select their own.

BIRTHDAY PARTY—A WISHING WELL

We may rejoice and be glad all our days.

A WISHING WELL THEME will appeal to all ages. For the young folks it has an air of mystery and excitement because the young *know* wishes will come true. For older folk, a Wishing Well party can be very beautifully planned and the theme holds a shiny hope for good days ahead.

INVITATIONS

Our invitations will be little wishing wells. You may find a picture to look at as you sketch this. Cut the well from folded construction paper. Color the bottom of the well or the foundation part to look like stone or brick. The slanting roof over the top could have little red shingles to give a touch of color. From the top, tie a brown string and attach a bucket cut from folded paper. Paste the sides of the bucket, leaving the top open to hold your folded invitation. You might write something like this: "Please come to Mary's house, Wednesday at 7:00 o'clock to help make her birthday wish come true."

DECORATIONS

You will surely want a Wishing Well for your party. A small brown keg could form the well. Add two thin boards on either side to support a roof. An old orange crate could make a slanting roof. Cover it with "brick type" crepe paper which would look like shingles. Make the well more colorful by entwining vines and tiny flowers around the boards which support the roof. You may place the birthday gifts in the Wishing Well. The well must have a shining bucket hanging from the top. This bucket could hold balloons, suckers, or other favors for the guests.

Your birthday table too must display a Wishing Well for a centerpiece. For this, you may use a coffee tin covered with brown paper. Place two sticks on either side of the can to support the roof. (Small nails will hold the sticks firmly enough to support your roof which will be made of a folded sheet of construction.) The bucket that hangs in this well may be a small nut cup. The coffee tin "well" may contain favors for the group.

Miniature Wishing Wells for each place may be made from brown nut cups. Dark pipe cleaners may be used to support the roof which is fashioned from construction paper. Cut a tiny bucket from aluminum foil.

GAMES

This Is What I Wish for Your Birthday

Each person is to write the name of the birthday person on paper and wish for him something beginning with the letters of his name. For example, if the name were **Mary** you might write, "I wish Mary, Many A Rich Year."

Wishing at the Well

Small children are sure their wishes will come true! Give each a shiny penny to toss at the well. You might use the larger Wishing Well or the one that was your centerpiece if you play this *after* you eat. Have the older ones keep their wish secret. However, you may ask them to toss a penny and reveal their birthday wish for the honored guest. No doubt a group of teenagers will make some hilarious wishes for the person honored.

Wells from the Bible

The Bible makes many references to wells. How many of these do you know?

1. God promised His people "houses full of all good things, which thou filledst not, and wells digged, which thou _____ _____." (Diggedst not)

2. David longed for a drink of the water from the well at _____. (Bethlehem)

3. Proverbs says: "Drink . . . and _____ _____ out of thine own well." (Running waters)

4. "The mouth of a righteous man is a well of _____." (Life)

5. Solomon speaks of a fountain of water, a well of _____ _____ and streams from Lebanon. (Living waters)

6. Jesus says the water He shall give will be a "well of water springing up into _____ _____." (Everlasting life)

7. Isaiah says that "with joy shall ye draw water out of the wells of _____." (Salvation)

8. Jesus met the woman of Samaria at _____ well. (Jacob's)

9. The woman of Samaria told Jesus the well was _____. (Deep)

10. Peter speaks of a time when there are wells without _____. (Water)

BIRTHDAY PARTY—MOTHER GOOSE

ONE OF THE FIRST SOCIAL ACTIVITIES in which a child participates is a birthday party. It may be his own or one for his friend.

Before you begin your plans, may I make a few suggestions? As you well know, tiny youngsters—two- or three-year-olds—any preschool child, in fact—are not completely adjusted socially. Such a child may be very frank or extremely shy. So let us keep this in mind as we make our plans.

Most preschool children are acquainted with the Mother Goose nursery rhymes so we shall use that theme for this party. If you do not have a copy of a Mother Goose book on hand, better get one and "read up."

INVITATIONS

Mary's little lamb is familiar to children so cut a lamb out of heavy white paper. Paint in the features and add a gay bow around its neck. Tie a tiny jingle bell to the bow. If you wish, you may cover the front of the lamb with cotton.

On the back of the lamb you might print an invitation something like this:

"This is Mary's little lamb. It wants you to come to Bobbie's house on April 24 at 2:00 and help him celebrate his birthday."

Or:

> Mary's little lamb says, "Come
>   To Bobbie's house at two,
> To help him celebrate his birthday
>   On April 24, oh, do."

You may mail the invitations but we have found that the children dearly love to take these invitations to their friends.

This may not be according to the best rules of etiquette, but it is fun and it leaves no doubt in the child's mind about his friends being "invited."

Do not plan rich or fancy refreshments for this party. Children like the foods to which they are accustomed. If it can be conveniently arranged, have small children come for lunch and then play an hour or so. This does not upset meals or nap routine. Plain wholesome sandwiches, carrot strips, and glasses of milk may be served. Cut the sandwiches with cooky cutters so they look fancy. Cut slices of cheese into little animals or other designs with cooky cutters. Glasses of milk may be served with colored drinking straws.

To all children, birthdays mean ice cream and cake so these are a *must*. Many of the children will want to blow out the candles and make a wish, so why not keep the big fancy cake for the family and serve individual birthday cupcakes to the children. Then every child may have a lighted candle to extinguish when the birthday child blows out his candle. There is something exciting and magical about a birthday wish and every child is sure his wish will come true.

Little ice-cream cone clowns may be served with the cake. Fill a pointed cone with a rounded scoop of ice cream and turn upside down on a plate. The cone is the clown's hat, the ice cream his head. Make his features of small candies.

Children always enjoy balloons so use a big balloon with the child's name printed on it in nail polish; mark his place at the table.

GAMES

You will want to have enough games planned to keep the children entertained but do not try to rush them from one game to another. I remember the time when Jean Marie helped a little friend celebrate his second birthday. The first game played was "Ring Around Rosie" and that was all the children would play all afternoon. We mothers tired of it,

but the youngsters were still enthusiastic when it came time
to go in for refreshments.

Mary's Little Lamb

Tell the children Mary's little lamb ran away and they are
to try to find it. Have enough lambs hidden so each child
will find one or two, at least.

Jack Be Nimble

Let the children say the familiar nursery rhyme. Then
draw a birthday cake on the floor and place a small candle
upon it. As the children say the poem they take turns jump-
ing over the candlestick.

Little Boy Blue

Let one child be little Boy Blue and the others be the sheep
and cows. When Little Boy Blue blows a horn (or whistle)
the other children run "out of the corn" to a certain base.
When a runner is tagged he too becomes a Little Boy Blue
and helps to catch the others.

Coloring the Cake

Give each child a large piece of brown wrapping paper and
let him draw and color a birthday cake. Give them a chance
to admire each others artistic efforts.

Rest Time

"Listening time" should follow an exciting time. Perhaps
you have some children's records that the children will enjoy. Ask them to sing the familiar songs. You may find a
little book or story and read to the children. It is fun to listen
to a story and share it with each other.

Prizes and Gifts

It is not usually satisfactory to give prizes to winners of
games. Small children will not understand why one child
should have a prize and not he. If you *do* give prizes, give

an award to all, but let the winner of a game get first choice as to color.

Do not be surprised if some child decided he does not want to part with the gift he has brought. Ask each child to *hide* the package he has brought and make the birthday child search for each gift. It really is not much fun to sit and watch one child unwrap a lot of gifts, so why not bring out favors for each child at this time.

Present the gifts or favors in such a way that the guests have fun too. Tie strings to the packages; give a string to each child and let him follow his colored string to that gift. Or hang a sheet and let the child "go fishing" for his gift. He drops the fishing pole over the curtain and while he is waiting for a "nibble" you attach an appropriate prize to the hook.

Even older children like a Jack Horner Pie which can be easily made by covering a large round pan with crepe paper. Ribbons are tied to the gifts and only a piece of the ribbon extends through the top of the pie. Pink ribbons will distinguish gifts for girls, blue ribbons for boys. When the boys and girls are ready to open the pie, have them repeat:

> Little Jack Horner
> Sat in a corner;
> Eating his Birthday pie.
> He put in his thumb—
> And pulled out a plum—

And at that phrase all the children pull out their gifts.

If the children have come to the party unescorted, you may find them reluctant to leave at an appointed time. To send them hurrying straight home, give them a little mystery package tied securely. Give them instructions that the package is to be opened "when they get home." You might put some candy, crayons, pencil sharpener, or other small gift in the package.

These parties are a very important event to the child and his enjoyment will repay you for all your efforts. If possible, take pictures, and later share them with all the children.

MISCELLANEOUS GAMES FOR ANY PARTY

Indoor Scavenger Hunt

IF YOU HAVE PLANNED an outdoor scavenger hunt and the weather forces you indoors, here is a good substitute. Give each person or each team a list of items he is to collect in his sack. These are hidden indoors, and the first one to find all the items or the one who has found the most when time is called is winner. You might include straight pins, safety pins, any kind of costume jewelry, pencils, bobby pins, erasers, needles, string, pen points, corn, beans, rice, peas, thimbles, clothes pins, wrapped candies, keys, toothpicks, crayons, shoe-string, buttons, corks, and various other small objects.

Getting Acquainted

These stunts will help everyone to get acquainted. Stand in a circle and tell each person that in one minute you will start around the circle and each person must tell the name of the person on his right.

Form two circles so that the players are facing each other. When the music plays, one circle moves to the right, the other to the left. When the music stops, you speak to your partner, tell each other your name, your school or occupation, and your hobby.

Seasonal Word Game

This game may be played in spring, summer, autumn, or winter. If your party is in the spring ask each person to write as many words as possible starting with *S* and ending with *G*. For example, sing, song, sting, stag, etc. At a summer party the words would start with *S* and end with *R*. In autumn, the words start with *A* and end with *N*, and in winter start with *W* and end with *R*.

Scriptural Squares

This is one of the most interesting games played; it is suitable for all ages and for a small group or a large crowd. You can adapt it to seasons by covering the squares with candy hearts for February, candy corn in October, tiny paper Christmas trees in December, and thus for any month.

Make your squares from heavy cardboard and mark off into spaces—five across and five down—similar to a Bingo card. In the squares print names used in Scripture for Bible characters. Each card must be different. The caller has all of these names on small cards so he can call them. As the name is called, that player covers the square if he has it on his card. The first player to cover five squares horizontally, vertically, or diagonally, or in the four corners and centers is winner.

Here are some names you may use on your cards: Eve, Adam, Cain, Abel, Seth, Methuselah, Noah, Ruth, Boaz, Naomi, Hagar, Lot, Gideon, Peter, Saul, David, Joseph, Manoah, Elisabeth, Mary, Cornelius, James, John, Onesimus, Isaac, Abraham, Absalom, Ishmael, Ahaz, Jezebel, Zerubbabel, Balaam, Barak, Jael, Bathsheba, Eli, Samuel, Samson, Delilah, Esther, Mordecai, Haman, Jonah, Daniel, Jude, Job, Lydia, Malachi, Nehemiah, Michael, Leah, Rachel, Rebekah, Onan, Zimri, Paul, Rhoda, Aquila, Priscilla, Eunice, Lois, Hezekiah, Joshua, Ezra, Jeremiah, Isaiah, Ezekiel, Mark, Matthew, Luke, Timothy, Titus, Philemon, Amos, Obadiah, Reuben, Judah.

Cross Out the Word That Is Out of Place

1. Moses—boat—burning bush—arrow   (Arrow)
2. Noah—commandments—ark—Flood   (Commandments)
3. David—coat—harp—giant   (Coat)
4. Joseph—dreams—lions' den—colored coat   (Lions' den)
5. Samuel—temple—coats—bulrushes   (Bulrushes)
6. Absalom—thick hair—beauty—wisdom   **(Wisdom)**

7. Aaron—priest—burning bush—rod   (Burning bush)
8. Elijah—chariot—bear—ravens   (Bear)
9. Solomon—riches—wisdom—golden calf   (Golden calf)
10. Daniel—fiery furnace—lions' den—tower of Babel
    (Tower of Babel)

Match the Fathers and Sons

Fathers	Sons	Answers:
1. Abraham	a. Joseph _____	(1—g)
2. Adam	b. Esau _____	(2—e)
3. David	c. Jonathan _____	(3—h)
4. Manoah	d. Japheth _____	(4—f)
5. Jacob	e. Cain _____	(5—a)
6. Isaac	f. Samson _____	(6—b)
7. Noah	g. Isaac _____	(7—d)
8. Saul	h. Solomon _____	(8—c)
9. Jonathan	i. Samuel _____	(9—j)
10. Elkanah	j. Mephibosheth _____	(10—i)

Who Am I?

Find the letter of every word,
To spell one who served the Lord.

		Answer:
1.	Found in *some* but not in *one*;	(S)
2.	Found in *Dan* but not in *done*;	(A)
3.	Found in *my* but not in *you*;	(M)
4.	Found in *us* but not in *two*;	(U)
5.	Found in *eve* but not in *night*;	(E)
6.	Found in *light* but not in *sight*.	(L)

Who Am I?

		Answer:
1.	Found in *see* but not in *tree*;	(S)
2.	Found in *one* but not in *three*;	(O)
3.	Found in *live* but not in *dive*;	(L)
4.	Found in *four* but not in *five*;	(O)
5.	Found in *mire* but not in *tire*;	(M)

6. Found in *fore* but not in *fire;* **(O)**
7. Found in *men* but not in *guys;* **(N)**

The answer is a man so wise.

Who Said It?

Here is a list of famous quotations. Who said each one?
1. "Am I my brother's keeper?" _____ (Cain)
2. "Few and evil have the days of the years of my life been." _____ (Jacob)
3. "To obey is better than sacrifice." _____ (Samuel)
4. "Whither thou goest, I will go." _____ (Ruth)
5. "I find no fault in this man." _____ (Pilate)
6. "The Lord is my shepherd." _____ (David)
7. "Lord Jesus, receive my spirit." _____ (Stephen)
8. "Christ Jesus came into the world to save sinners of whom I am chief." _____ (Paul)
9. "She gave me of the tree and I did eat." _____ (Adam)
10. "Take me up and cast me forth into the sea." (Jonah)
11. "I am slow of speech and of a slow tongue." _____ (Moses)
12. "Where is the lamb for the burnt offering?" _____ (Isaac)
13. "My son, God will provide himself a lamb." _____ (Abraham)
14. "Behold the lamb of God which taketh away the sin of the world." _____ (John the Baptist)
15. "I will go." _____ (Rebekah)
16. "Let us sell him to the Ishmaelites." _____ (Judah)
17. "The Lord gave and the Lord hath taken away." _____ (Job)
18. "Give me now wisdom and knowledge." _____ (Solomon)
19. "What must I do to be saved?" _____ (Jailer)
20. "Mine eyes have seen thy salvation." _____ (Simeon)
21. "Whomsoever I shall kiss, that same is he." _____ (Judas)

22. "If thou hadst been here, my brother had not died."
_____ (Mary)

23. "Thou art the Christ." _____ (Peter)

24. "God will surely visit you and ye shall carry up my bones from hence." _____ (Joseph)

This quiz may be lengthened by asking the person to identify the occasion for saying these famous lines.

Magical Letters on the Stairs

Draw squares on paper and fill in only first letter. Give Bible references and see who can fill in squares first.

Town in Moab—Numbers 21:28
Good king—II Chronicles 14:2
Prophetess in Jerusalem—Luke 2:36
One of David's mighty men—II Samuel 23:8
Husband of Priscilla—Acts 18:2
Companion of Paul—Titus 3:12
City of priests—Joshua 21:18
Famous box—Matthew 26:7
Nomadic tribe—I Samuel 15:7

A verb—John 3:3
From end to end—Exodus 26:28
A god worshiped—II Kings 17:16
Where language was confused—Genesis 11:9
He saw an angel with a sword—Numbers 22:31
Captured Jews—Jeremiah 39:1
Preached at Antioch—Acts 11:22
Home of Philip and Andrew—John 1:44
Blind beggar—Mark 10:46

144

Identify the Biblical character with the object. **You may** use some real objects—others will be pictured.

1. Basket _____ (Paul)
2. Scarlet thread _____ (Rahab)
3. Rooster _____ (Peter)
4. Star _____ (Wise Men)
5. Needle _____ (Dorcas)
6. Salt _____ (Lot's wife)
7. Rod _____ (Aaron)
8. Ladder _____ (Jacob)
9. Colorful coat _____ (Joseph)
10. Arrow _____ (Jonathan)
11. Rainbow _____ (Noah)
12. Garden _____ (Adam)
13. Gourd _____ (Jonah)
14. Bones _____ (Ezekiel)
15. Lions _____ (Daniel)
16. Sling shot _____ (David)
17. Bag filled with coins _____ (Judas)
18. Nail and hammer _____ (Jael)
19. Purple cloth or dye _____ (Lydia)
20. Small bush (tinted red to represent burning bush) _____ (Moses)

Helping Johnnie

Johnnie tried to tell a story at school but he got confused. Can you help?

One day Johnnie's father bought him a _____. (Genesis 47:17)

Johnnie kept his present in the _____. (Job 39:12) Sometimes he took it to the _____ (John 10:9) where there was plenty of _____. (I Kings 18:5)

He gave it plenty of _____ (Mark 4:28) and nice cool _____. (Proverbs 25:25)

He had to buy a new _____. (Psalm 32:9) He got some new _____ (Job 16:13) too.

One day his father bought him a beautiful new _____ (I Kings 13:13) trimmed with _____ (Malachi 3:3) and many pretty colored _____. (Isaiah 61:10)

ANSWERS

Genesis 47:17—Horse
Job 39:12—Barn
John 10:9—Pasture
I Kings 18:5—Grass
Mark 4:28—Corn
Proverbs 25:25—Water

Psalm 32:9—Bridle
Job 16:13—Reins
I Kings 13:13—Saddle
Malachi 3:3—Silver
Isaiah 61:10—Jewels

Who Am I?

Pin the name of a well-known Biblical character on each person's back. Each must try to identify himself by asking questions which may be answered only with "Yes" or "No."

Magical Squares

How many four (or more) letter words can you write using the letters in the squares and without crossing any other squares? You may go up or down or diagonally but do not omit a square. Here are a few of the words it is possible to spell.

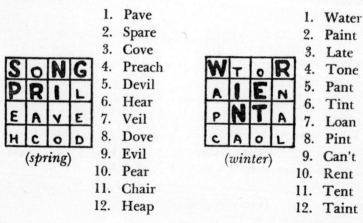

(spring)

(winter)

1. Pave
2. Spare
3. Cove
4. Preach
5. Devil
6. Hear
7. Veil
8. Dove
9. Evil
10. Pear
11. Chair
12. Heap

1. Water
2. Paint
3. Late
4. Tone
5. Pant
6. Tint
7. Loan
8. Pint
9. Can't
10. Rent
11. Tent
12. Taint

146

Can You Name the Books of the Bible?

1. Money due rot _____ (Deuteronomy)
2. A man test lion _____ (Lamentations)
3. Pen him lo _____ (Philemon)
4. Reveal it on _____ (Revelation)
5. Ah nee him _____ (Nehemiah)
6. O I bad ha _____ (Obadiah)
7. Cars hit no in _____ (Corinthians)
8. Veil is cut _____ (Leviticus)
9. Gal is a tan _____ (Galatians)
10. O Sam _____ (Amos)
11. Eli Dan _____ (Daniel)
12. Us lame _____ (Samuel)
13. He rest _____ (Esther)
14. Slaps m _____ (Psalm)
15. E hear Jim _____ (Jeremiah)
16. Oh sea _____ (Hosea)
17. I C Ham _____ (Micah)
18. Ah claim _____ (Malachi)
19. Wheat mt _____ (Matthew)
20. Ransom _____ (Romans)

PARTY GAMES

To the zoo you'll merrily go—
How many animals do you know?

1. He is sure footed as you can see.
   On a mountain he will be.
   —I Samuel 25:2 _____

2. If the weather is hot and dry
   This one still can always get by.
   —Matthew 19:24 _____

3. Give him little oats and hay
   And he will work for you alway.
   —Exodus 15:21 _____

4. He is stubborn—that is true,
   Can this as well be said of you?
   —II Samuel 18:9 _____

5. He is small, and fast, and sly,
   You may see him if you try.
   —Song of Solomon 2:15 _____

6. He will pace, and roar, and rage—
   I'm so glad he's in his cage.
   —I Samuel 17:36 _____

7. Black or brown or maybe white—
   Either way his claws're a fright.
   —Hosea 13:8 _____

8. She is gentle—just chews away,
   And gives us food for every day.
   —Isaiah 11:7 _____

148

9. He is docile—does no harm,
   And his coat will keep you warm.
                   —John 10:3 _____

ANSWERS

1. Goat	3. Horse	5. Fox	7. Bear	9. Sheep
2. Camel	4. Mule	6. Lion	8. Cow	

By the Dozen

Below are a dozen numbers. Look up the references and find the object each number designates.

1. One _____ Ephesians 4:5   (Lord)
2. Two _____ Mark 12:42   (Mites)
3. Threefold _____ Ecclesiastes 4:12   (Cord)
4. Four _____ Ezekiel 1:5   (Living creatures)
5. Five _____ Luke 12:6   (Sparrows)
6. Six _____ Exodus 20:9   (Days)
7. Seven _____ Matthew 18:21   (Times)
8. Eight _____ John 20:26   (Days)
9. Nine _____ Luke 17:17   (Lepers)
10. Ten _____ Luke 19:13   (Servants)
11. Eleven _____ Exodus 36:14   (Curtains)
12. Twelve _____ Matthew 10:2   (Apostles)

RECIPES

Party Punch

Basic Fruit Punch—30 small glasses

1½ cups sugar
2 cups strong tea
1 cup lemon juice
5 cups orange juice

2 quarts ginger ale
Orange and lemon slices to
float on top.

Sherbet Punch

Make the above recipe but add scoops of sherbet and pour the ginger ale in last.

COOKIES

Cookies can be served at almost any type of party—even at the fancy teas. Here is a tasty cooky that is ideal for cutting into holiday shapes for decorating.

Sugar Cookies to Cut

1 cup butter
2 cups sugar
1 teaspoon vanilla
½ teaspoon lemon

3 eggs, beaten
½ teaspoon salt
4 cups sifted flour

Mix ingredients in order given. If the batter should seem a trifle stiff, add a few drops of milk. Chill about half an hour. Roll about ¼ inch thick and cut. Bake on ungreased sheet at 400° from 8 to 10 minutes.

Crisp Butter Cookies

1 cup butter
1 cup sugar
¼ teaspoon salt

1 egg
2 cups sifted flour
½ teaspoon soda

Shape into rolls and chill. Bake at 400° for 8 to 10 minutes.

Easy Boiled Frosting

This boiled frosting sounds too easy to be true—but *try it*.

1 cup powdered sugar
5 tablespoons water
1/4 teaspoon cream of tartar

⎫
⎬ Bring to boil and boil
⎭ one minute.

Add flavoring (your choice)
Pour slowly over one stiffly beaten egg white. Spread over cake.

Heavenly Hash Topping

Use this as colorful topping for angel food cake.

1 egg	8 cut, colored marshmallows
1/3 cup sugar	1/2 cup drained crushed pineapple
2 1/3 cups milk	
Pinch of salt	1 1/2 cups maraschino cherries
3 tablespoons quick-cooking tapioca	1/2 cup cream, whipped

Beat egg thoroughly, add sugar slowly until mixture turns golden colored. Add milk and salt. Cook over low heat, stirring constantly, until mixture comes to a boil. Cool and stir occasionally. Fold in marshmallows and pineapple. Chill. When ready to serve fold in whipped cream and cherries.

Topping and Filling for Angel Food Cake

2 cups water   1 cup sugar

Boil 20 minutes. Remove from heat but while hot add one box orange Jell-o. When partly set, whip mixture. Add 1/2 pint whipped cream and 1/2 pound colored marshmallows cut very fine.

Cut angel food cake crosswise twice. Put this mixture between layers and over top of cake. Leave in refrigerator over night.

Easy 1-2-3- Frosting

1 tablespoon cocoa   3 tablespoons flour
2 tablespoons powdered sugar

Mix ingredients; then add any hot liquid until the right consistency to spread. May use hot milk, coffee, or fruit juices.

SPECIAL PARTY FOODS

Chili suppers are fun in cold weather. After an evening of coasting or skating or after the football game, you might bring the gang in for chili. Steaming bowls of chili, crackers crisp from the oven, and a relish tray, will be all you need.

Chili Soup—for six

3 tablespoons fat   ½ teaspoon salt
2 finely chopped onions   ½ teaspoon pepper
1 pound ground beef   ¼ teaspoon chili powder
1 can kidney beans   ¼ cup catsup
1 No. 2 can tomatoes

Melt fat, add onions and fry. Add meat and cook until browned. Add beans, tomatoes, catsup, and seasonings. Simmer 30 minutes.

PARTY SALADS

A good salad can add a touch of color to your refreshments as well as being a delightful taste treat.

Three-Layer Salad

You may vary the flavors of gelatin and thus select the color "theme" you desire. This is made in three separate pans first.

(A) 1 package cherry Jell-o
     1 cup boiling water
     1 can whole cranberry sauce
     ½ cup chopped nuts

152

(B) 1 package lemon Jell-o
     1 cup boiling water
     1 3-ounce package cream cheese
     1 9-ounce can crushed pineapple

(C) 1 package lime Jell-o
     1 cup boiling water
     1 cup grapefruit juice
     1 cup grapefruit sections

Mix A, B, C separately. In each, mix the Jell-o and boiling water and allow to cool before adding ingredients. Chill each mixture. When it is just ready to set, put into a pan in layers.

This is very colorful served on lettuce leaf, topped with a bit of salad dressing and a cherry or half of stuffed olive.

Brownies Deluxe

2 eggs, well beaten	½ teaspoon baking powder
1 cup sugar	2/3 cup flour
½ cup salad oil	1 teaspoon vanilla
½ cup cocoa	½ cup walnuts
½ teaspoon salt	

Beat eggs and add sugar. Mix thoroughly. Add oil and cocoa; mix. Add the sifted dry ingredients and mix. Add vanilla and nuts. Pour into greased tin and bake at 350° for about 30 minutes.

Cut these into squares and top with rounded scoops of ice cream. Choose sherbets or ice cream in flavors to carry through any desired color scheme.

Chocolate Cups for Ice Cream

To make a chocolate cup for ice cream, melt a 6-ounce package of semisweet chocolate bits and 3 tablespoons butter over hot water. Stir until well melted. Put this chocolate into paper baking cups and swirl around until the cups are well lined. Put in refrigerator until chocolate is firm, then remove the paper.

Fill these chocolate cups with ice cream, top with a strawberry or maraschino.

Dazzling Dessert

This dessert is so rich, you can serve it with a drink and it will be sufficient refreshments. You may vary the flavors of gelatin to carry out any color scheme you wish. This is a very pretty dessert and so good!

1 package orange or lemon Jell-o (or a combination)
1 package cherry, raspberry, or strawberry (or combination)
1 package lime
1½ cups hot water for each package
1 envelope plain gelatin
¼ cup cold water
1 cup hot pineapple juice
½ cup sugar
1 teaspoon vanilla

Dissolve each package of gelatin in 1½ cups hot water and chill separately. When firm, cut into very small cubes—about 1½ inches.

Soften gelatin in ¼ cup cold water and dissolve in hot pineapple juice. Cool and fold into 1 pint whipped cream to which add ½ cup sugar and vanilla.

Blend cubed gelatin into whipped cream mixture. Turn this into a large pan lined with this crust:

Crust

Mix two dozen crushed graham crackers with ½ cup soft butter and ½ cup sugar. Press 2/3 of this mixture into pan, cover with the whipped cream mixture and top with the remaining 1/3 crumb mixture.

Chill and serve.

Note: This sounds complicated when you first read it. However, it is very simple to make and so pretty and tasty.

Yummy Date Pudding

1 cup sugar	⅛ teaspoon salt
½ cup milk	1 cup chopped dates
1 cup flour	1 cup black walnuts
1 teaspoon baking powder	

Mix and put in a long pan and pour the following mixture over batter:

1 cup brown sugar
1 tablespoon butter
2 cups boiling water

Bake at 350° from 30 to 40 minutes.

Frozen Strawberry Dessert

Dissolve in double boiler:

16 marshmallows
2 tablespoons strawberry juice

Cool slightly and add:

1 cup crushed strawberries
½ cup crushed pineapple
1 3-ounce package cream cheese

Add: ½ cup salad dressing
Fold in: 1 cup whipped cream
Mix, put in tray, and freeze. Does not need stirring.

Popcorn Balls

Popcorn balls are a great favorite at any party. They may be transformed into jack-o'-lanterns or other characters by using gumdrops or jelly beans for features. Or the popcorn can be pressed into Christmas tree molds—or any others—and used at various parties. You may tint the syrup and carry out certain color schemes.

Sometimes you may mold the popcorn ball around a sucker and thus the children have something to hold to and also an extra treat of candy. You can also surprise your guests by wrapping a small gift in waxed paper and concealing it inside the ball.

Here is our favorite recipe:

3 quarts popped corn	2 tablespoons butter
1 cup molasses	1/4 teaspoon soda
2/3 cup brown sugar	2 tablespoons vinegar
1 cup water	

Boil all ingredients except soda until a thick ball forms in cold water. Remove from fire and add soda. Mix well and while foaming, pour over corn. Makes 18 good-sized balls.

Caramel Corn

Caramel corn is delicious and so easy to prepare.

> 2 cups sugar
> 1/2 cup boiling water
> 1/4 teaspoon cream of tartar

Stir together and boil slowly until it turns a light brown. Remove from fire and add 1 tablespoon butter and 1/2 teaspoon soda. Pour over 5 quarts popped corn. Set pan over low fire and stir until corn is well covered.

Fudge

Candy makes a hit at any party. And a "kitchen" party is a grand idea for entertaining the young folks. Let them don aprons and hit for the kitchen.

This recipe for fudge is an all-time favorite. It can be kept in a plastic bag for several weeks and remains moist. This makes a large batch.

> 4 cups sugar
> 1 14½-ounce can evaporated milk
> 2 packages chocolate chips
> 1 pint marshmallow creme
> 1 teaspoon vanilla
> 1 cup walnuts, if desired

Boil sugar, milk, and butter together to soft-boil stage. Requires almost constant stirring. Remove from fire and add chocolate chips, marshmallow creme, and flavoring. Stir until well dissolved, then add nut meats. Pour into large buttered pan. Chill.

Butterscotch Nut Fudge

This is a truly delicious, different kind of fudge.

½ cup butter
2 cups brown sugar, firmly
  packed
2 cups granulated sugar

1½ cups sour cream
2 teaspoons vanilla
1 cup black walnuts

Melt butter in heavy pan. Add sugars, cream, and mix well. Cook to 240° or soft-boil stage. Remove from heat and add vanilla. Let stand until almost cool then beat until mixture loses its gloss. Add nuts and pour into buttered pan.

Peanut Brittle

1½ cups raw peanuts
1 cup sugar
½ cup water
1½ tablespoons butter

½ cup corn syrup
¼ teaspoon baking soda
½ teaspoon lemon flavoring

Spread the peanuts on shallow buttered tray or cooky sheet. Mix sugar, syrup, and water, stirring until sugar is dissolved. Boil without stirring until mixture is *very* brittle when tested in cold water or boil to 300° on candy thermometer. Remove from heat, add butter, soda, and flavoring. Pour over the peanuts making a thin coating. When cool, break into pieces.

Molasses Candy to Pull

Nothing is more fun than an old-fashioned taffy pull.

½ cup butter
2 cups sugar

1 cup molasses
1½ cups boiling water

Melt butter in heavy kettle, then add remaining ingredients and boil to soft-boil stage or 230°. Turn into buttered pan and as mixture cools around sides, fold in toward center. When cool enough to handle, pull until light colored. You may add a few drops of oil of peppermint or wintergreen. Butter hands so candy does not stick. Cut into small pieces with knife and place on buttered plates to cool.

MAKE YOUR OWN SUNDAES

It is fun to let your guests make their own sundaes. Start with scoops of vanilla ice cream and let them take over from there. Besides the various toppings provide marshmallow creme and finely chopped nuts.

Fruit Toppings

Fresh or frozen strawberries, raspberries, or even peaches may be chosen.

Chocolate Sauce

½ cup light corn syrup
1 cup sugar
1 cup water
3 1-ounce squares unsweet-
ened chocolate

1 teaspoon vanilla
Few drops walnut flavoring
1 cup evaporated milk

Cook syrup, sugar, and water to soft-ball stage. Remove from fire and add chocolate squares and stir until melted. Add flavorings. Slowly add evaporated milk. Mix well and store in refrigerator. This may be reheated in a double boiler for hot fudge sundaes.

Caramel Topping

Melt one pound of vanilla caramels with ½ cup water in top of double boiler. Stir until smooth. May be used hot or chilled.

Peanut Butter Topping

Mix peanut butter with just enough hot milk to make the right consistency for spooning over ice cream.

FAVORS ·

Let's Make a Corsage

Flower gardens provide hours of fun in making floral arrangements but if you have never tried making corsages, you are overlooking another source of enjoyment. With a few simple steps you can turn almost any blossoms into a corsage to brighten up your own outfit or use them for gifts or favors.

You will need to purchase some florist wire and tape. These are inexpensive and go a long way.

Select substantial bright blooms and place them in cold water for awhile as soon as they are cut. Cut stems short and push wire through the stem of each flower. For a delicate flower extend the wire through the blossom, make a tiny hook, and pull the wire back so the hook is concealed in the petals.

Wrap each stem in florist tape. Now place separate flowers in a pleasing arrangement and tape firmly together. Tie with harmonizing ribbon.

Place the corsage in a plastic bag and keep in refrigerator when not being worn.

Handkerchief Folders

Handkerchiefs are always welcome gifts, especially if you add a crocheted or tatted edging or a bit of dainty embroidery in the corner.

And the handkerchief looks even more attractive if you put it in a fancy folder which you can make very easily. Using construction paper, cut a piece about 4″ by 9″. Fold one end over so a pocket is formed deep enough to hold the handkerchief. Punch holes on each side of the "pocket" and tie with ribbon. Decorate the folder with original designs, decals, or gummed seals, or bright-colored pictures cut from magazines. Fold the hanky neatly and fit it into this folder.

These make attractive gifts for Mother's Day, for the teacher, or for club prizes. And a lovely all-white handkerchief would make a dainty gift for a bride-to-be.